Shetland Hap Shawl

Then and Now

Sharon Miller

493/2006
Sharon Miller
5th November 2006

Hap *: a warm covering – to wrap warmly*

"The Shetland hap shawl is often the first piece of Shetland Lace attempted by many a knitter, even though we may not know the pattern by that name at the time. It was the case with me and is so, and has been for many another for at least 150 years, and most likely longer than that.

When we see this shawl first dressed, we often begin an entrancement with Shetland lace knitting that leads us to go on to ever finer and more intricate pattern work. But it seems a pity that our first starting point should be so overshadowed; I and others love the hap in its many forms : workaday "stout", baby christening fine, or enchantingly shaded. Unlike finest Shetland Lace, the hap shawl has no recorded history as such and so this book is an attempt to give it both a tribute and a first context."   Sharon Miller

CONTENTS

A Shetland Mother and Baby
Courtesy of the Shetland Museum.

Right: Staff at D & G Kay's drapery store, in Lerwick, in a promotional photograph c1905. (From The Shetland Museum.)

Hundreds of dressed haps, both plain and patterned are piled in sizes behind, ready for sale. Many of these would be parcelled and sent down 'South' on approval. Kays supplied the best London shops including Harrods and Fortnum & Mason.

Despite the comparatively enormous numbers of haps made and worn locally, few original shawls are in textile collections today.

Inset (& Cover *Dressing Shetland Shawls*) **and Below:** This interesting pair of photographic postcards were both taken by J. D. Rattar and show what I believe to be his wife's relations, the Petrie family, at different times dressing shawls - one in the 1900s and one in the 1940s. To me, it looks as if they could even be located in the same yard in Lerwick. Lengths of smooth thread were strung through each shawl's border points, then these strings were tautened onto pegged battens to allow the shawl to dry under tension, they could be left like that in storage till needed too, often covered under the double bed. Usually, the maximum was about six shawls per frame.

The Petrie family dressed hosiery and ran a provisions store. From these we can see the effect the change in fashion had on the knitting trade – latterly, fine lace was still produced, as were haps, but by then, allover patterned colourwork jumpers and 'tams' (circular hats, the woman behind the lace shawl is holding one up) were much more popular and the hap shawl trade seems very diminished, judging from the presence of only one here.

Local knitting had a ready market in the Second World War as servicemen were stationed or stopped over in Shetland, and so bought knitting for themselves and as presents for their family members. Courting servicemen often complained that their Shetland girlfriends were "always knitting"!

Knitted Shetland Shawls – A Historical Context

It may seem odd to start a book on quite a humble shawl with a quick history lesson on fashionable layering, but I hope the reader will bear it, as it's important to some readers, and to me, to understand the evolution of an item: the "why and the how" it came about, to become comparatively to us, so important. But if you are a Knitter only, you may skip this part!

Shawls as such, may be seen essentially as a nineteenth century phenomenon. Before this, and in chronological order, the main term for loose, decorative or practical outerwear seems to be: **Mantles (with many spellings, earliest recorded reference: Old English)**, which were high status sleeveless wraps before 1200, but vulgarised as the centuries passed so that these became seen as ¾ length versions of the cloak, for example:

> **c 1385 Chaucer** *The Knight's Tale*: "A *mantelet* upon his shoulder hangynge Bret ful of rubies rede"

Cloaks (c 1275) from about this date, were full length blanket-like squares gathered and tied at the neck, either with or without hoods to cover the body from shoulder to foot. As variants to cloaks, there appeared **Capes (1560/70s)** and **Whisks (1654)**, these were usually waist-length cloaks and again, these were normally sleeveless. Additionally, there were stole-like **Wraps (1460? Used as "wrap" in context as dress: 1827; "Wrappers" - 1782)**; and **Tippets (c 1300)** which were long tasselled scarf-like lengths, originally for clerics only it seems. By the 1700s, there were other pretty shoulder/breast coverings such as the large, diagonally-folded square **Kerchief (1300** French: "couvre-chef" – head/hair cover**)** and its close relations, the **Neckerchief (1382,** see drawing, page 9**)** and **Handkerchief (1530)**. Then, there was the **Partlet (1515)**, a version of this was known as a **Tucker (1688)** because its ends could be tucked into dress fronts for modesty or warmth. All these unfitted coverings could be used both practically and decoratively:

> **Abraham Tucker** writing **1768 - 74**: "When, on looking through the window, we see the women pulling their *handkerchiefs* over their heads, we take this for a sign that it is beginning to rain."

> **Betsy Sheridan's journal**: *Letters from Sheridan's Sister*, **1786**: "The *hankerchiefs* are not so much puff'd out and there is now a very pretty sort of hankerchief* much worn open at the neck and exactly made and trim'd like a Boy's shirt."

Other small forerunners of the shawl as a head-covering were **Wimples (c1100)**; **Head-rails (Old English)**; and possibly "Showers": as found under entry for Neckerchief in the *Oxford English Dictionary* - and still in use as a term for a light covering in the USA. Earliest use, if so: **1382**, Douce "Pynnes and sheweres and necke couercheues and filetes." (*SM: This in modern English could be "bonnets", "showers"[?], "neckerchiefs", and "head bands"*). More definitely, and more intended for covering shoulders too, there were **Crisps (1397)**; **Stoles (Ancient:** frequently ecclesiastic in earliest contexts; but used first in English as description of less "ceremonial" dress – **1725)**; and **Scarves (1562)**:

> **Thomas Hudson, 1584**: "Upon her head a silver *crispe* she pind, Loose waving on her shoulders with the wind."

> **Robert Green** writing **1593** *Mamillia*: "Needless noughts, as *crisps* and *scarfs*, worn a la morisco."

> **Samuel Rowlands 1600** *The letting of humours....* : "Why in the Stop-throate fashion doth he go With *Scarfe* about his necke?"

Then there were late-coming descriptions of similar but flimsier French shawl-type items: the **Buffon (1750)** which was worn to "puff out the breast" in other words, to make the bust seem fuller as a curvy silhouette was in fashion; and the prettily trimmed, triangular *Fichu (1803) which may be what Betsy Sheridan was describing above. The word **Shawl** (derivation possibly Persian, perhaps named after the first place of manufacture**) is first recorded as such as late as 1662 in English, when Indian goods were introduced through growing trade links to Asia:

> **John Davies** (of Kidwelly), **1662**: "The richer sort have ..... another rich Skarf which they call Schal, made of a very fine stuff, brought by the Indians into Persia." *(SM: This is most likely a Cashmere product.)*

At first, "Kashmir" or "Indian" shawls were treated as the costly and much admired ornately hand-woven or embroidered textiles they then were; and as such used for light decorative furniture coverings and counterpanes (just as carpets had first been used in Europe in the 15th and 16th centuries) before ladies took them up for themselves as daily decorative wear; probably in the mid-1760s. Shawls soon became especially worn as high fashion accessories for the classically inspired lighter shift dresses of Regency costume and later fashions, where their drape effects could be shown to advantage: see right, an illustration of evening dress from *Ackerman's Repository, Jan. 1825*. These imported prestigious shawls were soon imitated in Europe by Jacquard loom weavers and lace makers, and so became enormously popular. By the 1860s and 1870s shawls of all kinds and materials were at their zenith, as they were thought particularly suited for wear over crinolines and bustles:

> "the outdoor article *par excellence* for our changeable climate is the shawl….Graceful and *dégagé*, the shawl will retain its place in our *toilettes* when the ephemeral costumes and fancy dresses are forgotten or laughed at ….." *Englishwoman's Domestic Magazine, 1869*

** **"I next came to the city of Shaliat, where the shaliats are made, and hence they derive their name."** *The Travels of Ibn Batuta* **Rev. Samuel Lee, London, 1829. Ibn Batuta (c 1307 – 1377) was a Muslim geographer. Shaliat seems to have been a large fine city/port near Calcutta. Other recorded place names are Chalia, Chalé, which closely correspond to perhaps earlier shawl names included in this list: schal, shawool, sallallo, shell, shalie, saloo, châle, cheyla. All could be Europeanised forms.**

On the other hand, researching typical working women's clothing before tourist photography has been very difficult. Much more attention is given to fashionable clothing, the wearing of which obviously defines the status or 'class' of the wearer through time and so its new appearance as we have seen, is traceable through the many portraits of the rich or famous; or in writing. But in the past as now, as soon as a particular fashion item becomes widely copied and available to the less rich it loses covetable status - be it a Kashmir Shawl then, or a certain designer handbag now, and so drops from notice. However the point I'd like to make is that once, that item <u>was</u> fashionable, <u>was</u> talked about, pictured and described; so, even though it may eventually have become "workaday", costume historians have the potential to trace its history from first appearance to decline; for example, the ruff collar of Elizabethan England.

With working women's clothing, this is not the case! It seemed so ordinary and unchanging to the contemporary writer or artist that it rarely attracted pre-1800 interest and so there seems strikingly little recorded change for centuries. When one does find an illustration of early female Scottish dress for example, it is normally of the *Arisaidh:* a woven, often striped or tartan large rectangle, belted round the waist in its middle to form a full long skirt with the lower half and a "shawl" with the top half brooched together at the neck or shoulder; or worn over the head, see below. If not of the arisaidh, pictures seem always to depict a similar skirt, and if visible, a blouse, short jacket or cloak. Laced bodices in one form or another may feature too from the 16th to the early 19th centuries. Chequered plaids are also recorded, see illustration, inset.

In the Highlands, it's important to note that the wearing of historic Scottish costume for men – known then as Highland Clothing: of tartan, plaid (as worn by the man in this illustration) and kilt, was strictly banned after the Jacobite Rebellions in 1747; but with a neatly malicious twist, the ban did not extend to its being worn by the King's hated soldiers as part of their uniform. Infringement of this ban was first punishable by six months' imprisonment and then by transportation for a second offence, the ban lasted for over 30 years.

Prints of 1740s Scottish costume showing the Arisaidh, the "Jupp" and plaid – inset. *Le Costume Historique - Ecosse* **A. Racinet, Firmin-Didot, Paris, 1876.**

What happened at that time with the women's arisaidh is less clear; but it seems most likely that in Shetland, under Scotland's and therefore Britain's control at this time, everyday clothing either had or increasing became more like that of the Scottish Mainland, and most especially to that of neighbouring trading ports of the 'South' (Mainland Scotland) such as Newhaven, near Edinburgh. The first descriptions we have seem to show this – for example, by the early 1800s, Shetland fishermen were shown typically as wearing oilskin jerkins or tunics made from leather, trousers, knit-frocks and long-tailed knitted hats or knitted striped bonnets; but this dress too was in transition, Dr S. Hibbert, c 1820, writing of Shetland:

"The boat dress of the fisherman is, in many respects striking, and picturesque. A worsted covering for the head, similar in form to the common English or Scotch nightcap, is dyed with so many colours, that its bold tints are recognised at considerable distance, like the stripes of a signal flag. The boatmen are also invested, as with a coat of mail, by a surtout *(SM: tunic/overcoat)* of tanned sheepskin, which covers their arms, and descends from below their chin to their knees, while, like an apron or kilt, it overlaps their woolen femoralia *(SM: his term for leg coverings)*: for, with the later article, it is needless to observe, the Shetlander is better provided than the Gaelic Highlander. The sheepskin garb has generally an exquisite finish given to it by boots of neatskin *(SM: calfskin)* materials, not sparing in width, reaching up to the knees, …. There can be no doubt that this leathern dress is of Scandinavian origin; a similar one is still worn in the the Faroe Isles……. This ponderous and warm coriaceous *(SM: "leather")* garb is, however, sometimes disdained by the younger and more hardy natives, who content themselves with a common sea jacket and trowsers of the usual form, and, in place of the worsted cap, with a plain hat of straw." *quoted p 726, Guide to the Highlands.*

Before the 1700s in Scotland, undyed wool was made into a coarse homespun grey cloth called "hodden" for common wear. By the 1770s, with the arrival of cotton, the woven material for local working women's clothing is recorded as drugget - a strong and warm locally-woven cloth of "wool with linen or cotton". This could be made into pretty striped clothing, usually of white or yellow, with red dyed stripes as shown above. Drugget, or "linsey-wolsey" (a wool/linen cloth) was favoured for hardwearing skirting and most likely worn up to and after the 1900s; it's shown frequently in photographs taken in the late 1880s around the Scottish Highlands and Islands. Regarding outer layers, an Ayrshire minister Mitchell, writes in the 1780s (post-ban) of plaids of varying qualities being worn by all classes of women and, in particular he confirms the countrywoman's dress too, as being by then mainly of striped drugget skirts:

" 'strong and serviceable rather than fine … (with) … a short gown fitted closely to the bust or upper part of the body and commonly called a 'jupp'." *quoted p 96 Scottish Costume 1550 – 1850, Stuart Maxwell and Robin Hutchison.*

This description is supported by L. Lettice: *Letters on a Tour* 1792, describing women's local dress in Ecclefechan, a village just over the Scottish border, near Gretna:

"…………..the short jacket and pettitcoat of two different colours, and the square chequered wrapper or cloak, the covering of the more ordinary women, prevailed in the dress of the more elderly people; the younger person of both sexes shone in a tawdry imitation of their southern neighbours." *Quoted p 102, (ibid).*

These descriptions are further supported by two contemporary artists, David Allen and Alexander Kay:

"A cap of cotton or linen, surmounted by a stout napkin tied below the chin, comprises the investiture of the head; the more showy structures wherewith other females are adorned being inadmissible from the broad belt that supports the 'creel', that is, fishbasket, crossing the forehead, A sort of woolen pea-jacket, of vast amplitude of skirt, conceals the upper part of the person, relieved at the throat by a liberal display of handkerchief. The under part of the figure is invested with a voluminous quantity of petticoat, of substantial material and gaudy colour, generally yellow with stripes, so made as to admit of a very free inspection of the ancle, and worn in such immense numbers. One half of these ample garments is fastened up over the haunches, puffing out the figure in an unusual and uncouth manner, white worsted stockings and stout shoes complete the picture." *Alexander Kay's notes, c1830s. Quoted p 125-6, (ibid).*

This costume worn by Newhaven fishwives, was likely to have been widely current and later pictures appear to show such similarities, see page 6. The costume historians Maxwell and Hutchison note that the painted idealised views of the 1780s such as *Scotch Wedding* and *Highland Dance* by David Allan, show folded kerchiefs; the ends of which are tucked into the wearer's bodice. Other country girls are shown with triangular kerchiefs (small shawls) crossed in front over dresses of printed cotton – a material which appeared in the early to mid 1800s. Large rectangular woven plaids (not then a term just applied to tartan) as coverings for men and women are shown in the contemporary paintings of Alexander Carse which feature Scottish country dress of the early 1800s. In his *Mauchline Holy Fair* fine quality shawls appear amongst the Regency fashions, and prominent is a scarlet hooded-mantle, along with other shawls and plaids of varying qualities; and one woman sits wrapped with a large red plaid covering her head and back. His *The Open Air Preacher* repeats the scene, with wrappers of fine materials worn as shawls and kerchiefs; and large red plaids are worn over heads again, or carried by even comparatively well dressed members of the audience. Interestingly for us, a nurse with a toddling baby is shown wearing a white triangular kerchief/shawl with a single thin blue stripe near its borders' edge.

Focusing in on Shetland, *The Court Books of 1614 –15* mention black French cloth and thefts of a 'sewit sark' (shirt), a 'wob' ('web' – woven length) from a workloom and also of a belt and an 'auld plaid' (old plaid), which gives an idea of clothing at that point. Moving on, the earliest illustrations of Shetlanders (c1820) show costumes similar to those recorded in the rest of Scotland at that time. One entitled *Shetlandais* in a French book, shows a young woman knitting a sock on a set of needles and wearing a long full skirt to ground with a close-fitting, long sleeved jacket to her waist, perhaps the jupp or "jupe". This jacket has a low neckline, from which her white underlinen peeps upward to her throat. She also has a triangularly folded head-square which is knotted at the back of her head, with every strand of her hair tucked in. It's obviously a tranquil fair weather scene, so gives no record of the potential use of shawls. Headwear often denoted if a local girl was married or single: frilled "mob" caps with long tying ribbons, known as 'mutchs' in Scotland, were normally worn by married women or widows then; and this as we shall see, remained much the case well into the 1930s in remoter regions. During the 19th century if not before, in some Scottish islands it became traditional for a girl wore a bright shawl to show she was unmarried. I now conjecture that as fine woven linen or cotton cloth would always be a comparatively expensive item requiring to be purchased, not grown or home-made, Shetland women would try to make such "kerchiefs" as one of their own articles of knitting from at least as late as the early 1800s; not so far as I've seen, listed for sale then as were their hats, gloves, frockcoats and stockings, but it's feasible to me. There is tenuous evidence from 1840 and 1861 to back this:

1840 : "I met one cleanly dressed chatty old gossip, the sort of looking personage who hobbles on the stage at the beginning of a farce, exclaiming, 'How my old bones do ache!' and she assured me with great exultation, that she manufactured a stocking per day, and that every article she wore was entirely of her own spinning. I liked to see her honest pride, and if the gown had been French cambric, she could hardly have expected me to admire it more."

p 104, Shetland and the Shetlanders, Catherine Sinclair.

She comments too, that Shetland men exchange their knit stockings for Dutch sailors' clogs. It's entirely possible that the woman she met had had her homespun yarn woven into a soft cloth called 'wadmel' – a woollen cloth that in Shetland dated back to Viking days. (Catherine Sinclair was the

***Shetlandais*, a print from *Region Circumpolars* in unknown French geography book, 1820 - 1840. The hand-colouring of this engraving is at least slightly inaccurate I believe, in that the men's knitted caps should be brightly striped, see Dr Hibbert's quote page 2, and photograph, next page. It's likely too I think, that the knitter's skirt should be striped.**

diary-keeping daughter and secretary of "Agricultural Sir John" Sinclair who worked tirelessly as president of the Highland Society. He instigated the collection of the unprecedented Statistical Account of Scotland c 1790, with a view to improve the lot of the poorer people and in particular those of his own lands of Caithness and in neighbouring Shetland.)

And **1861** : "Until within the last 15 or 20 years knitting for sale in these islands was confined to stockings and seamen's coarse frocks; the remainder of the wool was home-made into blankets and stuffs for common wear." *The Poor Knitters of Shetland, A Lady Resident, (Eliza Edmondston), Paisley, 1861. Quoted p 72, Linda G Fryer.*

It would be impractical after all, to wear let alone make, knitted wool skirts; and any night linen would double for day wear. But the women's own woollen stockings were home-knit, as were their men's 'frokes' (sweaters) and caps, and the men's waterproof tunics were home-sewn of sealskin or cowhide until about 1860. Wherever possible, regional clothing was home-made; and therefore it seems more than reasonable that the origins of Shetland knitted shawls started as home produced clothing. One thing Shetland had in abundance since Neolithic times was sheep, with fleece of a very soft fine quality; ideal for knitting, and so almost all Shetland women had spun and knitted for centuries. The finest wool was ideal for luxury knits though too soft for durable body clothing, so this was made into stockings, caps and gloves for trade and the coarser wool utilised more at home. Perhaps prototypes of the knitted hap were a development on the (woven 'wadmel') blankets mentioned above; doubly invaluable as they could be quickly donned and so elastic through being knitted not woven, that they could tuck a babe in close, or be quickly pulled up to protect the woman's head against wind and rain. This double function of clothing wasn't unusual, the Scotsmen's "plaidy" was both their dress and their blanket – see Appendix 2. (Interestingly, this was customary well into the 20th century when for example, poor Eastender families in London often used their coats as extra blankets.) Another significant advantage to a knitted blanket/shawl is that it wouldn't need weaving: almost all Shetland women with yarn had knitting skills and 'wires', few had free access to looms.

In a Hebridean watercolour in Alexander Kay's *Portraits from Nature* 1812, the "guailleag", Gaelic for "shoulder shawl" is shown. This was a regional item of dress – possibly of Viking origin or earlier in form and use. I believe similar clothing must have worn in Shetland as forerunners of the hap, and an interesting sidelight comes from archaeological digs such as at Oseberg, Norway, where discoveries indicate that some of the earliest ancestors of Shetland, Viking women, frequently wore shawl-like rectangles (as plaids, perhaps?) over their heads and shoulders; most likely as weather protection as well as for status and ornament; these important functions hap shawls later performed in Shetland, when for example, a black hap showed a woman was a widow.

A *Shetland Interior* of a hundred years ago. We can see the grandmother in her mutch (bonnet) near her spinning wheel, and the younger woman bending over the new sewing machine. Clothing was invariably made at home as much as possible for the vast majority of Shetland households as elsewhere. The man wears his knitted fisher cap and the woman at the sewing machine wears what seems very likely to be a small undressed hap or shoulder shawl – I've had the magnifying glass on it! (See page 49, for method of dressing / blocking.) In the picture we can see a small stool and a cloth cowl over the open fire. This popular postcard image was later turned into a coloured drawing and used by The Singer Sewing Machine Company as an advertisement. The child seems to be holding a 'tushkar', a tool for cutting peat.

Note: These early postcards are often of quite poor image quality, but the things we can learn from them are extremely informative. Even allowing for the fact that they are often specially composed, they are still quite representative of their content; a decision we can make by comparing them with each other and with other source material. So, after making allowances for certain degrees of artistic licence, we can still rely on these for a fair amount of accuracy.

To date, the exact origins of the Shetland Hap shawl are not yet, and perhaps never will be, firmly established, but Shetland women in the early 1800s were shown laden with 'kishies' of peat or even manure – see page 7, a chore that must have been done for centuries. They would therefore require a protective layer over their backs and heads to help mitigate basket movement, discomfort, mess, and so on, that doing such work in a rainy, windy, northern climate would cause.

As noted earlier, the contemporary woven kerchief of the late 1700s – 1900 was frequently embellished with a prominent striped or chequered border – such as that shown right and next page; importantly for us, the last is shown worn by an old country woman, presumably wearing a fashion of at least a generation or two earlier. I propose that a Shetland knitter in trying to copy that once fashionable stripe effect for a blanket / kerchief / evolving hap shawl, would devise the method of making four identically striped borders united by a plain garter stitched centre, the form that became so typically Shetland. To support this view, we must look more closely at this famous approach to shawl construction, to see what we can reasonably deduce from that.

Traditionally and strictly speaking, a Shetland Hap was made of nine knitted pieces:-

4 edgings + 4 borders + 1 square centre, see right:

I prefer to think of it as "5 pieces" myself; as in reality, the four borders are knitted onto their foundation edgings. As said, I believe this method of piece-by-piece knitting was conceived to make it possible to knit striped bordered shawls. And this piecing had a direct and vital bonus in that "stout" (this has to be another word for hap) shawls could be made whilst walking; a practice noted in late-contemporary travellers' descriptions. The earliest precise reference I've yet found is the following from an anonymous, but presumably male author, who is perhaps understandably given this era of early tourism, much more taken with exciting sea voyages, staggeringly beautiful coasts and bird-catching than in describing the domestic life of Shetland women, other than (and for us, importantly) the briefest mention of what he sees unusual:

"There is perhaps no community that gives such indications of industry among the female population as Shetland. The knitting needles and the worsted are continually in their hands, and seem to form part and parcel of the woman herself.

"If you take a walk towards Tingwall, you will meet or pass dozens of women going for or returning with peats from the hill, all busy knitting – one a stocking, another a stout shawl or cravat.* The finer articles – scarfs, veils, and lace shawls, which are often exquisitely fine – cannot be worked in this offhand way, and are reserved for the leisure hours at home."

p214, Half-Hours in the Far North: Shetland. A world-wide series for Young Readers published by Wm. Isbister Ltd., London, 1883. With accompanying illustration of the costume of the 'better class' of Shetland children.

This is, I must emphasise, my own theory as a knitter, but would explain the otherwise unusual complexity of this manner of (continued page 8.)

Above:
Line drawing *'lady with fan'* Ingres, showing a fashionable bordered kerchief, c 1800.

Below & Right:
The pieces of a Shetland hap – the edged borders would stretch to fit around the centre square when dressed.

GIRL AND BOY OF THE BETTER CLASS.

* 'cravat' was also a term to describe a small knitted neck-scarf for either a man or woman during the Victorian period.

Scottish & Regional Dress in the 19th Century

The images on this and the next page show the marked resemblances between British Regional and Shetland working dress. The indoor scene below (c1900s) is very like that typical of a Shetland croft of the 1890s, and the worker appears to be making slippers of woven strips of material. It's interesting to note her fringed shawl has coloured banding very similar to Shetland haps and is probably a woven forerunner of the knitted hap - this costume is very like that also worn in Shetland. The woman wears a 'mutch' which usually denoted a married woman or widow, so does the Orkney spinner.

Newhaven Fishwives " Three Generations "

Newhaven, near Edinburgh c1900, there are similarities of form between the Arisaidh and this, see page 2.

A Cromaty Fish Hawker c 1920

Cromaty is a tiny fishing port of the East Scottish Highlands. Her clothing is strikingly like that of Shetland thirty years earlier.

HIGHLAND COTTAGE – INTERIOR.

Orkney Spinner c 1910

Spinning, Orkney.

Skye Crofters, c 1920 striped skirts again!

Highland Courting c 1910

THE SPINNIN' WHEEL.
HIS WORDS INTO HER HEART DID STEAL
BUT AYE SHE TURNED HER SPINNIN' WHEEL.
Photo-Braid.

Irish linen spinning c 1900

Cornish Fishwife c 1890

Shetland Dress in the 19th Century

images c.1890 – 1920
see also, images of Shetland spinners and knitters throughout.

Words in 'single quotes' in this book are usually Shetland terms.

Carrying 'kishies' of peats, 1901, Gremista: oddly, no one's knitting, perhaps the weather's too wet or cold; or the hill is too steep. Note coarse aprons or top skirts folded back to create pockets. Women on left and right seem to be wearing haps, the woman in the centre seems to be wearing a tattered woven shawl.

Left: This toothless older spinner of c 1920 wears a mutch with strangely quite modern printed cotton clothing, although her skirts are still striped. Note the sack of fleece she seems intent on spinning. The tools of her work are arranged at her slippered feet: Under the 'cairds' lies an 18 inch /45cm H - shaped (niddynoddy) or 'hesp tree' for winding spun yarn into 'cuts' (hanks) of 100 threads of 2 yards each. The two bobbins ('pirms') mounted together are for folding - plying - finer spun singles into a plied yarn.

Right: A more fashionable young woman carding, wearing the 1880s leg-o'mutton puffed sleeves. Note the traditional, practical apron and striped skirts are still present.

This indoor scene (c 1900) is that of a croft interior showing box beds left and right. Fish and meat is smoking above the hearth. Here, we can see the small can paraffin lamp ('strupi') hanging above the fire that would provide light to work by. Note the light small hap of the woman carding, and the "plaid" square of her companion, meaning here the tartan-like woven shoulder shawl.

(continued from page 5) shawl construction; a form which would be simple to think up for a knitter with advanced skills in the shaping of socks and gloves. A 'pieced-up' method of construction for me becomes in turn an important point, when one thinks of other knitted folk shawls of the same period and before, such as Orenburg Shawls or those similarly knitted as Orenburgs – e.g. Estonian, Feroese shawls. These are all typically whole single or "one-piece" shapes such as triangles, rectangles or squares. When the first Shetland lace shawls appear they follow the Shetland "4 borders + centre" typical hap construction we'll come to recognise, and not the simpler one-piece form (meaning: "cast on to desired width and knit to desired length – with or without edging"). So for me, this is important evidence of a well-established Shetland tradition of shawl construction/design going back earlier than 1836/7, which is the date of the earliest known Shetland lace shawl. It seems logical that the first Shetland lace knitters would use a familiar technique of shaped shawl pieces they were fluent with to ground the new motifs in, and this has to indicate an established tradition of knitted striped or even lace* shawls - what we know of as 'haps'. It's crucial to understand that one wouldn't employ such shapings if one wasn't trying to imitate a coloured stripe and/or knit directional lace - after all, Orenburgs and other early lace shawls show that it's perfectly easy to do symmetrical lace motif patterning in even very large and fine one-piece shawls. I contend that if Shetland lace was a direct "copy" of Orenburg lace as has been suggested, the knitters would've used that one-piece technique at least initially, and most likely for long enough for it to be noted; and Eliza Edmonston, an interested local knitter writing within 20 years of that "first" Shetland lace shawl, couldn't trace a link to any external influences and credits the Shetland knitters themselves. As to the 'Old Shell' border that is such a defining feature of the typical Shetland Hap, the lace knitting pattern itself was once claimed by a local family to be one of only a handful of truly Shetland patterns (Richard Rutt, p.175) and it must have been one frequently knitted in their stockings for sale, similar to that shown below, from *Weldon's Practical Knitter* c1910. There is not more I can add to clarify this, except that in *Mary Thomas's Book of Knitting Patterns*, there is a photographed sampler of bonnet-back medallions (p. 237) recorded as "early eighteenth-century" and one (2nd column, 3rd row), though not clearly shown, seems to be in this pattern. I think the actual sampler is continental and therefore would show the pattern was known of there - if I am correct in identifying it as such and the sampler is genuinely early 18th century; it's known as "Peacock's Feather" (*Pfaufeder*) in Germany, one of the many countries Shetland had trade links with - including indirectly Spain - a "cradle country" for knitting. Perhaps dating such samplers with modern techniques will more firmly establish this pattern's origins; though there's no denying that it could have been independently invented in Shetland, once one explores the "delayed decrease patterns" such as Razor Shell, Old Shell, Ostrich Plumes, etc; it's easy to come up with "new" variations only to see them already in old pattern manuals!

Finally, I must now stress the importance of how it was the direst of financial circumstances that directly led to this overwhelming local reliance on knitting in Shetland, one that could only be met by almost endlessly knitting whilst doing domestic tasks or farming work as well as in their "leisure" hours. Famed for fine stockings since the 1600s, the knitters and their families had become increasingly dependent on the extra income from the women's knitting as time went on, a trade that was badly affected when stockings began to be made on knitting frames in the late 1700s. By the 1800s, poor harvests, war and taxes had fostered a system were many local women had to knit for their landlords and merchants for survival – they knitted whatever they could and bartered the knitting for small necessities or clothing, often getting deeply in debt. (Payment in goods -'truck', was illegal and in 1872, a Royal Inquiry was made, extracts are in Appendix 3. It's from this we gain invaluable insights into the truly harsh conditions of some of the knitters' lives. Although the Inquiry did lead to more cash payments, the system lingered on to the 1940s). Maybe for haps in the earliest days, a square garter-stitch knitted version of the blanket referred to earlier, could have been simply trimmed with a coloured stripe border made of yarn oddments, or a trial lace pattern; but this would involve a "Borders Outwards" knitting technique with the centre part having been made first – so, I believe that the "five piece" shawl construction utilized so famously in Shetland could be most easily explained by their knitters' well documented economic need to be constantly knitting and doing chores: it's obviously much easier and less risky (to the knitting) to do the four small edged border pieces individually, as the knitter walked, than to work a full size one-piece shawl straight off. In this way, the finished size of a border piece would be equal approximately to a stocking, something Shetland women habitually had knitted for centuries. As the stocking trade died for them, they relatively quickly took up and developed the fortuitously newly fashionable lace and shawl trade we recognise. We now can turn from the historical context and probable background of the Shetland hap to Shetland shawls themselves.

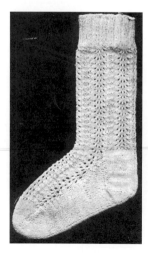

CAUTION! I truly hope readers will have noted how I have hedged my thoughts in this section with markedly careful wordings of "perhaps"; "for me"; and "I believe"; and so on. This interesting subject now has to be left open: scientific dating and research into other early European knitted shawls and samplers, and with luck, Shetland archaeology, will uncover dateable knitted artefacts that will fill in some of the blanks and turn my conjectures either into certainty or firmly rejected theorising.

*It's only for shawls with striping, and with directional lace patterning such as Old Shell, Old Spanish Lace, Razor Shell etc, that one needs separately knitted borders. Richard Rutt shows a fine 19th century Azores Lace Shawl (Spanish) in his acclaimed *History of Knitting*, page 118; but it seems from the text that this piece may well post-date the Shetland tradition, and may have indeed been inspired by it in part, again as a trade in knitted articles in local fibre to sell to the first tourists. It could well be a useful area for further research, but I will say that the borders on that triangular shawl are knitted vertically - by this I mean knitted up the "V" sides of the centre rather than at right angles abutting to it; this is a technique that isn't normally used in Shetland knitting, and the patterns in it, rely on delayed decreases to form fan-shapes rather than the Orenburg and Shetland "paired decrease/increase" way of creating motifs.

Victorian Knitted Shetland Shawls

For approximately seventy years, up to c 1920, Shetland knitters could exploit a comparatively huge market demand for their shawls along with their other luxury hand knits (see *Heirloom Knitting, 2002*); allowing them both to utilize the excellent quality of their wool and to derive vital additional income from this trade. The Shetland shawls knitted then can be divided into two main typical groups; those for everyday wear and those destined for fashion.

Broadly speaking, the thicker '*worsted*'* everyday shawls are mainly represented by the **haps,** and the luxury lace gossamer shawls by what's now known today as **ring shawls** but then as lace. The coloured postcard *Washing and Dressing Shetland Shawls* from c1900 above, neatly illustrates these two groupings of the "fashionable" and the "everyday" shawl classes, the dresser wears her hap, the lace shawl intended for sale is stretched to dry; another coloured hap is being washed in the tub. I must mention that the lace shawl dressed here is not of the highest quality, I have recreated it in a Shetland Cobweb 1 ply with a patterned centre. The finest gossamer yarn shawls were many times more exquisitely fine and more complex in pattern, as can be seen by this rare postcard below of c1920, advertising the *Shetland Wool Articles knitted by Mrs Mouat & Her Daughters* of Haroldswick. (Unst, where, reputedly the finest lace work was made. This card is published by William Mouat, also of Unst - so it looks as if family enterprise is at work!) Here, we can see a Hap Shawl, left, two Long Shawls (also known in the 1800s as 'Plaids', see page 55), a Veil or possibly a Fall (top centre, a small lace rectangle for attaching to hats or perhaps to be gathered around a neck), and a beautiful Lace Shawl. Crepe Shawls were "crossovers" between hap and lace shawls, as they were to hap pattern, but very much finer yarn, these were shawls normally intended for sale.

*thicker, tightly spun wool yarn.

From Sheep to Shawl

Knitting Shetland Shawls c1910, photographer: Thomas Kent, published in an article about Orkney by Maude Radford Warren in *Harper's Monthly Magazine* in 1911, though there were no text references to explain it. So, though possibly posed for in Orkney - the chair is a distinctive Orkney one with woven rush back, the height of the room is also a bit of a surprise, as is the clock; this purportedly shows an industrious hap shawl knitter at home with three representative haps. On the right of the wall clock, hangs a 'koli' (or 'kollie'), an open Shetland iron lamp developed from stone Viking ones. This burned fish, whale or seal oil. The oil would be poured onto a wick of dried rush pith or even twisted worsted wool yarn laid in the ratcheted top dish to create a lit flame about the same brightness as a candle. The lower dish caught any drips. The koli began to be superseded in the 1860s by the introduction of the paraffin lamp 'strupi' – see page 7. Lamps were essential for knitting during the long winter evenings.

Some of these photos make me smile – often the knitting shown "on the needle", is of a finished shawl because it is clearly fully dressed - as is this one, something not done until the entire shawl is knitted! However, it's interesting to note the wide lacy Three Hole Edging used with this white hap, pattern chart for that given on page 43.

Shetland Sheep ~ True Shetland Haps started from here!

Above: Shetland sheep (c1900) foraging on cliff-edge grass and seaweed, it's held that this sparse diet contributed to the especially fine quality of their wool. The sheep come in various shades of whites, greys and browns. *photographs above – Jack Rattar*

"The sheep in these islands look like goats or greyhounds, having long legs and lank bodies, and their colour is that peculiar brown and blue which the shetland stockings usually exhibit. Some are speckled of various hues, and go by the name of Jacob's sheep, though not lineal descendants of that flock." **Catherine Sinclair,** *Shetland and the Shetlanders 1840.*

Like the wild Soay, true ancestral Shetland sheep had a wool that each summer developed a "break point" allowing it to peel away. The Highland Society Report 1790, under the auspices of Catherine's father Sir John Sinclair, noted that Shetland sheep had the ancient characteristic of a two layer fleece: outer coarse hairs covering an undercoat of short fine wool that could be hand plucked ('rooed') in early summer, whilst the outer hair naturally moulted off in the autumn; and that as well as the hairier 'beaver' sheep, there were also 'kindly' sheep, with finer wool. There were then many attempts to improve the breed to increase fleece weight, etc.; in the late 18th and 19th centuries – some with disastrous consequences; and by 1882, Caulfield and Saward's *Dictionary of Needlework* refers to only the "Beaver Sheep". M L Ryder (1968) sees the modern Shetland sheep as an "intermediate" between the earliest Soay and the modern Cheviot. They were a tough breed, J C Spence and James Nicolson recorded that for winters, lambs were often taken in and fed hay, cabbage and potato; but adult sheep were left to fend for themselves, taking shelter from stone walls; or, if trapped in snowdrifts for long periods, even surviving by eating wool from each other. Nicolson also writes that it was usual that any stray tufts of wool ('hentilagets') were carefully taken from heather twigs and fences by the poorest women to use for their knitting; and that town knitters would make timely 'tigging for oo' visits to country relatives after rooing – thereby receiving small presents of fleece to spin up later when back at home. Rooing was a summer activity, and only in recent years have the modern-bred sheep been mechanically clipped, as the two layer fleece has been largely bred out.

Below: The softest neck wool ('haslok') was then hand plucked ('rooed') to ensure the maximum length of its staple, this precious wool made the finest spun gossamer yarn, while the body's coarser wool was used for the coarser knitting such as stout haps, or for weaving into tweed. Belly wool was 'aliplukkens'. I think the women are carefully wearing best clothes for this photograph!

Carding and spinning Shetland Wool.

A photographic postcard of c1905 showing Shetland spinning, in a subtle left-to-right narrative of the wool's processing.

Starting left, the spinning wheel perhaps has carded rollags or combings of rooed (hand plucked) wool draped ready for fine lace spinning. This wheel incidentally is a smaller upright Shetland wheel (Shetland: 'spinney'), said to be preferred locally because of its diminutive size, which better suited cramped life in a croft. In the 1760s, flax was a trial crop in Shetland in an effort to relieve poverty, and over 200 flax ('lint') spinning wheels were imported from Hamburg in readiness for spinning linen thread. Though the crops failed, the wheels were found to be good for very fine spun wool instead.

For ultra fine 2 or 3 ply lace yarn of 1000 yards per ounce and finer, Eliza Edmondston writing in the 1856 tells us that combing, and finger straightening, which untangled the precious long rooed hairs, was favoured over carding as it involved less breakage. As late as the 1890s and most probably later, wool combs ('kems': wooden handled rake-like tools with 10 fine-angled tines approx 6 inches / 15 cm long, set into a wooden bar of approx 4½ inches / 12 cm) were used to prepare finest lace worsted. The use of such wool combs is traceable back to mediaeval times.

Next shown, the girl is carding wool into "rollags" ('rowers') rolls of lightly oiled wool. Carding teased the hairs parallel by brushing them with the carding bats' surfaces which were densely covered with fine short steel pins. The wool could have been made ready by sprinkling with olive oil or a melted oily fish liver residue called 'gröt' (ref: *'Inga's Story'* J C Spence). Oils could be sprinkled by using a goose feather dipped in a pot. This work was dirty and arduous; to preserve the length of the carded hairs, the worker's arms would have to be repeatedly drawn back to their furthest, before the smooth backs of the wooden bats were used to gently roll the "roving"/ "slivers" or rollags. The girl wears a cotton head square to keep her hair clean.

The rowers were passed to the spinner to be drawn and spun into tightly spun worsted ('wirset') which was wound onto a bobbin ('pirn' or 'pirm'). Singles would have to be plied 2 or 3 fold to make a knittable 'thread', this was done by unwinding the singles from two or three pirms and 'twining' them together with the spinney onto another pirm. To complete, the yarn was hanked up onto an 18 inch niddynoddy 'reel' or 'hesp tree' see page 7, a full "figure of 8" wind on it would make a thread of 2 yards / 180 cm circumference). A hank was a 'cut' of 100 threads = 200 yds; see page 56. Each 'cut' was then tied to prevent tangling, then it could be wound into a ball ('cloo') for knitting ('makkin') with; or still as a cut be washed, and dyed or bleached, though a lot of the natural greys, red/browns and blacks came straight off the backs of the sheep.

The **Hap Shawls** pictured are interesting here: this 1900s hand-coloured version of the postcard has the girl's "piping stripes" of white on a light brown, see page 31, for its border colour chart. The woman's has white-edged banded shading of brown from dark to light to dark on a beige coloured shawl, very similar to the Morag shawl pattern shown on page 26.

Both these use the same traditional triangular edging as their foundation and both are knitted "Borders Inwards" – see next page. Note that when worn, the borders' lace holes curve downwards, like **BrIdges** (∩) in traditional "**B**orders **I**nwards" shawls as above, and upwards like **BOwls** (∪) in "**B**orders **O**utwards" shawls such as The Morag Shawl, page 26. I'll write in detail on these shawl methods next. What I want you to note now is how pinpointing the way the lace pattern arches is a useful tip to distinguish how a hap shawl was made.

"Borders Inwards" - Traditional Method

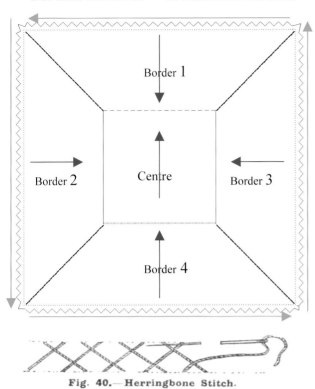

Fig. 40.—Herringbone Stitch.

"Borders Outwards" - Modern Method

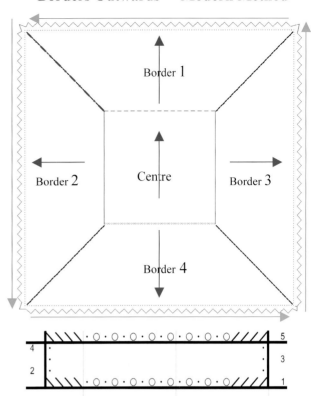

I describe in the following pages how 19th century Shetland shawls were made **Borders Inwards**, see above diagram left. This means a side edging was made to length first, then the archetypical Old Shell border of "lace hole columns" was made. This was repeated until there were four edged borders which were joined together with a plain (i.e. garter-stitched) centre square. The traditional White Hap Shawl on page 16, is made like this. It only needed the border "flap" side pieces to be Herringbone Stitched together, <u>or</u> Mattress Stitched (page 19), <u>or</u> closely sewn, to finish; this method is still used today.

But photographic evidence exists that as early as the 1880s – but probably much earlier - some knitters must have realised the advantage gained by making a shawl **Borders Outwards,** reversing the order of knitting by starting with the centre first and finishing with the edging. Richard Rutt refers to this construction as "Victorian Shetland". Most obviously, the main advantage was being able to knit in the round and not having to sew borders or do the grafting join of the centre to the border; the main disadvantage is that it requires the whole shawl to be worked on as one, and not in pieces. Another big plus is that the final size isn't fixed at the start, one can keep repeating border rows until it gets to a desired depth; unlike the traditional method where the perimeter edging is fixed first. (Red dotted line on diagram top right: see page 25's note.)

Although this construction may well have been done even earlier, I have not seen or read of anything yet that is further back in time than the 1880s. A photograph *Victorian Infant**, unmistakably shows a 2 ply single-coloured hap with a garter stitched <u>square</u> centre and with Old Shell <u>borders knitted outwards</u> (it seems to be made with 8 lace holes, patterning every 4 rows – see chart, above right) with a Six Hole Lace Edging, this was another frequently used Shetland edging, see page 43. The evidence of such a shawl predates the invention of circular knitting needles sometime four decades or so later**, so I presume that the knitter made the centre square on long, perhaps double-pointed needles, and then used each of the square's sides to make the individual border on, either singly or all together - see page 23. Next, if made separately, the four border flaps must have been sewn together, either before or after the edging(s) made. (Note: This is still a good way to make a shawl for knitters who either dislike circular needles, or don't yet feel confident to "knit in the round" with that method's drawback of possibly having to correct stitches in rounds that may well involve several hundreds of stitches.) The Morag, page 26, is a traditionally coloured hap, though my version is untraditionally, knitted "Borders Outwards".

A knitting pattern for the traditional "Inwards" hap is given on page 16, it is an exact replica of my original Shetland hap. Another "Inwards" hap, is on page 18, that's closely based on photographs of dressed shawls and a written Shetland pattern of the 1950s. Then, with a clear note that what follows regarding border colours has to be mainly deductions from a study of contemporary images, I give examples of several charted hap colourways, usually in natural shades as a reasonable working guide. These colourways have to be at best informed guesswork, as not many originals have survived - see next page; so I recommend serious students to examine as many original sources that can be found for themselves and to this end I have provided as many images as I can from my collection to assist with this. Other colour groupings can be used instead of the natural ones I give (e.g. blues); or a beautiful fine white or pastel shawl can be made with the instructions by using the same needle and approximately 250g of Shetland Cobweb 1 ply.

*East Lothian Museums Service, 2051 – Dr J T Richardson (photographer) Berwick. **The earliest reference for circular needles or "twin pins" in knitting magazine adverts that I've come across is from the 1930s, these needles had fine steel lengths of wire cable – they are both springy and unwieldy, I have several!

Hap Shawls

A Shetland Hap was and is, a serviceable warm shawl. The use of the word 'hap' in this sense, is mediaeval, meaning a "cover", or "to wrap snugly". Whereas the word dropped from English use after the 1500s, it was retained in Shetland and Scottish dialects, see Appendix 2. Hap shawls were one of the commonest articles of their own knitting (other than stockings) that later Victorian Shetland women used themselves, as well as making them for export. Haps, also known then and advertised, as "Wrap Shawls" and "Shetland Shawls", became preferred baby shawls and also the light bedcoverings of choice in many sanatoria, as the influential Dr Jaeger had been a strong advocate of the "medicinal" merits of woollens in the 1880s. Because haps were for everyday use, they were usually made in the thicker and often darker wools for durability and this had the benefit of enabling Shetland knitters to conserve the finer, rarer part of the fleece's wool for their lace knitting. Haps were then so very common and so little regarded, that despite the huge numbers made and worn locally in addition to those exported – see frontispiece of D & G Kay's Drapery store, few survive today in textile collections; the Shetland Museum has (at time of writing) less than a handful, and two of these are replicas.

Fortunately though for scholars of costume, the commercial popularity of haps coincided with the birth of photography and the first wave of mass tourism that required scenic postcards to send home; so knitted haps frequently appear worn in early postcard scenes of the Shetland Isles as well as in local photographs. Though woven squares were still frequently worn, by the 1890s, knitted haps became seen as the most characteristic outer covering for Shetland women and so were pictured worn in a variety of styles after being first folded on the diagonal into a large doubled triangle. Normally, they are worn with the shawl ends crossed over the breast and tucked into apron-bands; or knotted / pinned through at the front crossover. Sometimes, they are shown worn still as doubled triangles but with the ends crossed at the front then taken to the back to be secured under the shawl's points. Time and again, women are photographed with their shawls pulled up higher to cover their heads against weather or for extra warmth. By the 1900s, haps are shown folded into long rectangles and worn like stoles – again see frontispiece; as by then, stoles and scarves had begun to replace the fashion for square shawls.

Other articles of local dress recorded at this time were woven long striped skirts ('cots') worn with white or print blouses, aprons, stockings and 'rivlins' which were comfortable moccasin-like sealskin, or cowhide shoes laced over the ankle and foot by thongs – see Shetland postcards throughout, for further costume details.

From contemporary evidence then (photographs, price lists and *The Truck Report**), we can say that from the 1860s at latest, haps usually exploited the full range of local fleece colours (see inset) though dyed or bleached 'worsted' and other imported yarns were also used. Commonly, the hap shawls were knitted either in single colours of these natural undyed shades of greys, browns, blacks and cream; or with borders banded with arrangements of the other natural colours for contrast. Dyed pure white and pure red were considered suitable everyday colours – see postcard image below; pure black was reserved for mourning. The spun yarn for haps was normally of a medium weight worsted (equalling a modern '*jumper weight*': c 105m per 25g / 130yd per oz; dressed tension: 7 sts x 7 rows with UK 8 / 4 mm / US 5 - 6) and before starting, the knitter would allocate ounces and/or part ounces of colour for each hap. It's recorded that natural white haps were often afterwards dyed black or scarlet to rectify the yarn's natural imbalances in colour – see John James Bruce's evidence, page 55. Luckily, the illustrator Frank Barnard's *Picturesque Life in Shetland* provides us with an "artist's eye" of colours in 1890s haps. Obviously not familiar with knitting, he calls Old Shell lace on hap shawls "zigzags" and notes them as:

"double or treble, the stripes a delicate pink, blue or dove grey on a field of white; or coarser shawls with black zigzags divided by thin white lines, on a field of mouse colour, iron grey, or dark brown."

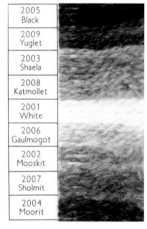

| 2005 Black |
| 2009 Yuglet |
| 2003 Shaela |
| 2008 Katmollet |
| 2001 White |
| 2006 Gaulmogot |
| 2002 Mooskit |
| 2007 Sholmit |
| 2004 Moorit |

The Shetland 2000 range of natural undyed wools with their dialect names: *Jamieson and Smith*.

*See Appendix 3

An artistically romantic scene of hap shawl dressing, c 1900:

A white hap is being dressed on a frame. One of the dressers wears a red hap in typical manner.

The stretched shawl is a larger version of one shown and written up on page 16.

Jessie and her mother Barbara Petrie are working haps, the sisters are working lace and colour work. I believe the hanks of coloured yarn are looped over Jessie's arm for effect: it's unlikely that she'd knit from them as an assorted group of coloured strands and her actual working yarn trails off picture. Note the empty dressing frame leaning against the wall on the left.

As late as the 1950s, haps were still sold in number from Shetland, e.g. from "Tulloch of Shetland"; but by then, these "miraculously light….cosy and protective" shawls were normally solely intended for baby wear and invalids, and so were then offered in what were considered appropriate colours, e.g. pale blue with white and lemon border bands (see page 31).

To knit a hap, customarily multiples of 'scores' of stitches (20 sts = 1 score) were calculated for each border's maximum - usually about "6 score" (120 sts, as for one shown next page) for a medium weight, everyday hap; though for the finer crepe shawls in a laceweight or gossamer yarn, the maximum could be as much as 23 score (460 sts) per side or more. Each hap border would usually be started with a simple 'lace' (edging strip) knitted for the shawl's intended length first - the edging itself would be started with a cast on of 7 to 12 stitches for 12 - 18 edging points. Then, the border stitches were picked up from this strip and the shawl knitted "Border Inwards" with almost invariably, an Old Shell patterning. The pattern rows for Old Shell could be as close as 4 or 6 rows apart, but more usually they were every 8 rows apart; this spacing depending on the knitter's or her family's preferred way of working, I'll give charts for all these later.

The use of coloured bands or not too, was usually at her discretion, though obviously governed by what yarn was available to her. After the four borders were made, a plain garter stitch square centre (invariably, I've noted, in the same colour as the edging) was used to unite the shawl borders. The shawl was finished by grafting the final centre's row to its border stitches and by sewing up the border seams before dressing. In addition, 'spotted haps' were recorded, where the centres had small patterns, whether these were of lace or small areas of cable stitch wasn't noted, though I've seen 1950s printed patterns for both. Perhaps rarer still, were 'fringed haps', these possibly had trailing fringes, instead of the decorative pointed knitted edge; but I suspect these would be more for trade than practical wear at home, or possibly they indicate just how closely the first knitted Shetland shawls followed original woven ones – see top left photograph, page 5. But long wool fringes are troublesome to keep tidy as well as time-consuming to make and so were quickly replaced by knitted edgings. One of the earliest and almost certainly a Shetland lace knitted shawl, was photographed in the 1840s. It had a long fringed variation of Old Shell border (Miss Rigby's Shawl, pictured page 14, Helen Bennett. Original: National Galleries of Scotland.) This large "Borders Inwards" lace centred shawl was definitely a highly fashionable one, but the haps we are to look at here were normally for humbler use as practical items worn to holes before being used as fuel for the fire. We'll next see that sort of hap.

A Shetland Peat Carrier. **Her knitting is tucked into the apron's waistband, the yarn may well be in a large apron pocket. Just visible under her elbow is a knitting sheath 'wisp' which was a tight bundle of straw tucked into the apron band for the sharp end of the double pointed long knitting wire to rest when not actually being knitted from. Using long double-pointed needles allowed knitters to achieve remarkable stitches-per-minute totals. Photo postcard: R H Ramsey.**

Shetland Peat Carrier

An Original Shetland Hap

Here is my vintage Shetland hap. I date this one to perhaps as late as 1960, it bears a *Shetland* quality label, which means it has meet the required standards for such an item. The pattern is given on the following pages, following the traditional method of "Borders Inwards" construction.

I think perhaps the most efficient way to make one of these at speed for the Shetland knitters of the c1860s onwards would be to make one edged border and continue knitting the centre square on that one when at home, meantime knitting the three other borders as she walked or worked outside. It was common though, for family knitters to work together on a shawl for quicker results.

The photographic postcard below, with its awful punning title is taken at Lower Brouster, Walls c 1894; and shows haps dressed on stringing to wooden pegs and pegged out on a hillside to dry like giant spiders' webs. Again, it is contemporarily hand coloured and so therefore we may reasonably rely on it for accuracy in showing colourways.

What is of particular interest to knitters though, is the wide variation in the sizing of the dressed haps – and the way some have been individually dressed to be relatively circular. Comparing this to the image shown in *Dressing Shetland Shawls* (frontispiece) we can see that a certain standardization of shapes and sizes must have taken place at some point for the shawls pictured later there to be lashed to fixed size, square frames. However, photos and other sources (e.g. W P Livingstone, page 178) show pegged out dressing for the odd shawl or shawls continued well into the 1940s.

Taken as a group here, the coloured haps' borders are almost all shown shading *dark-light-dark*, only one foreground shawl is shaded *light-dark-light*. I believe this is quite a good representation of the preferred colourway sequencing then. As shown here, many haps were single coloured, a lot had what I call "piping stripes" (Collection 1, first pattern, page 31). By the 1900s, the *dark – light – dark* banding on lighter or white shawls seems to be favoured over other colour arrangements.

A "Happy" Land (Shetland).

Pattern for a Traditional Shetland Hap

In Shetland Lace weight: 10 x 25g : 170m / 25g (approx 191 yd /oz) - this shawl weighs 250gm / 9 oz of one colour - **Please allow 10% extra to be safe!**

In Shetland Jumper weight: this would need 14.5 x 25g with same needle, but should make a bigger, warmer shawl. **Again, allow for 10% extra yarn!**

Note : Use Shetland wools for this method as they 'dress'/ block the best at the corners.

Needle 4mm / UK8 / US 5 - 6 : determine by measuring a dressed swatch.

Dressed Tension (US gauge) over garter stitch:
17 sts x 30 rows = 4 square inches / 10cm
Dressed Size: 52 x 52 inches / 132 cm square.

Hap Lace Edging

Cast on **11 sts**, then knit them back.
(These rows are shown below Row 1 on chart.)

Row 1 Wool round needle, k2tog., knit 7, make 1, knit 2. **(12sts)**

Row 2 Knit 1, k2tog., make 1, k2tog., knit 7*. **(11 sts)**

Row 3 Wool round needle, k2tog., knit 4, k2tog., make 1, k2tog., knit 1. **(10 sts)**

Row 4 Knit 1, k2tog., make 1, k2tog., knit 5*. **(9 sts)**

Row 5 Wool round needle, k2tog., knit 2, k2tog., make 1, k2tog., knit 1. **(8 sts)**

Row 6 Knit 1, k2tog., make 1, k2tog., knit 3*. **(7 sts)**

Row 7 Wool round needle, k2tog., knit 2, k2tog., knit 1. **(6 sts)**

Row 8 Knit 1, k2tog., knit 3*. **(5 sts)**

Row 9 Wool round needle, k2tog., knit 3. **(5 sts)**

Row 10 Knit 5*. **(5 sts)**

Row 11 Wool round needle, k2tog., knit 1, make 1, knit 2. **(6 sts)**

Row 12 Knit 2, make 1, knit 4*. **(7 sts)**

Row 13 Wool round needle, k2tog., knit 3, make 1, knit 2. **(8 sts)**

Row 14 Knit 2, make 1, knit 6*. **(9 sts)**

Row 15 Wool round needle, k2tog., knit 5, make 1, knit 2. **(10 sts)**

Row 16 Knit 2, make 1, knit 8*. **(11 sts)**

Repeat Rows 1 – 16 fourteen more times, see diagram right.

* = knit through the back of the last stitch of that row to "open" the loop made by previous row's "wool round needle" – shown by **star symbol** *on chart, right.*

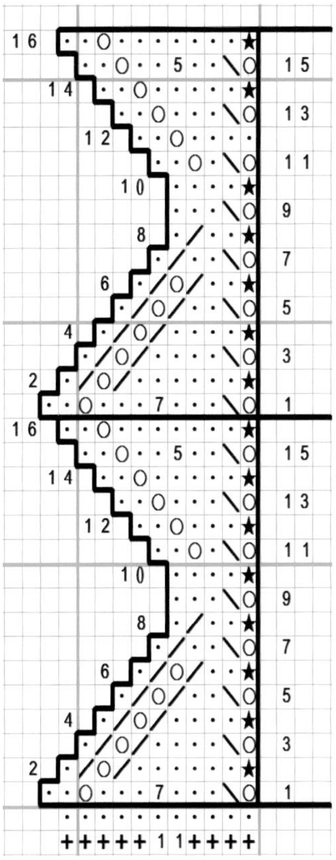

Lace Edging Chart

Shows 2 repeats of the 16 row pattern, to show 1 complete point.

When you've finished the lace strip, you'll have 14 complete points + two ½ points, one at the beginning and one at the end – see diagram. ➔

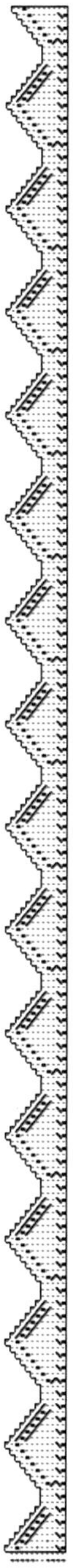

Border   *Diagram below shows a completed border*

From the edging's straight side "wool round needle": pick up (US "pick up and knit") into the back of each stitch to "twist" it = 120 sts "8 sts picked up per point" = 8 x 15 = **120 sts,** see picture on page 20.

Rows 1 & 2: increase invisibly into first and last stitch by "knitting into the front and purling into the back" of it.
(Row 1 : 122 sts; Row 2 : 124 sts.) Knit Rows 3 - 8

Hap Border Chart

------- see text, next page

6 Hole, 8 Row Old Shell "Borders Inwards": 81 Rows

Compare this Chart with the one on page 45 which has a lacier border pattern.

Star symbols = reserve sts or do Break Pattern for 4th border, see text.

1   2   3   4 (repeats of 19 sts)

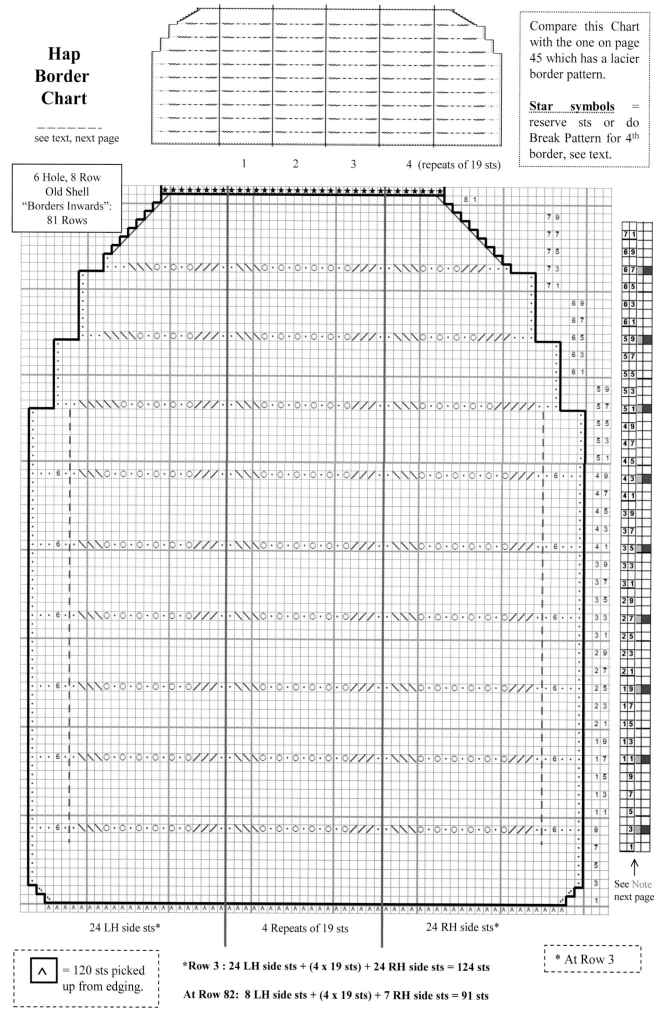

24 LH side sts*   4 Repeats of 19 sts   24 RH side sts*

∧ = 120 sts picked up from edging.

*Row 3 : 24 LH side sts + (4 x 19 sts) + 24 RH side sts = 124 sts

At Row 82: 8 LH side sts + (4 x 19 sts) + 7 RH side sts = 91 sts

* At Row 3

See Note next page

Border Pattern Rows

– – – – – – bar lines on chart previous page, show repeats that match exactly these directions up to Row 56.

Rows 9, 17, 25, 33, 41 & 49:

Knit 5, ***knit 1, (k2tog)3 times, (make 1, knit 1)5 times, make 1, (k2tog)3 times, knit 1**.**

Repeat from * to** to end, finishing knit 5.   **(124 sts)**

Row 57:

Knit 3, (k2tog)5 times, (make 1, knit 1)4 times, make 1, (k2tog)3 times, knit 1,

*knit 1, (k2tog)3 times, (make 1, knit 1)5 times, make 1, (k2tog)3 times, knit 1**.

Repeat from * to** to last 24 sts. Finish: knit 1, (k2tog)3 times, (make 1, knit 1)4 times, make 1, (k2tog)5 times, knit 3.

(118 sts)

Row 65:

Knit 3, (k2tog)4 times, (make 1, knit 1)3 times, make 1, (k2tog)3 times, knit 1,

*knit 1, (k2tog)3 times, (make 1, knit 1)5 times, make 1, (k2tog)3 times, knit 1**.

Repeat from * to** to last 21 sts. Finish: knit 1, (k2tog)3 times, (make 1, knit 1)3 times, make 1, (k2tog)4 times, knit 3.

(112 sts)

Row 73:

Knit 3, (k2tog)3 times, (make 1, knit 1)2 times, make 1, (k2tog)3 times, knit 1,

*knit 1, (k2tog)3 times, (make 1, knit 1)5 times, make 1, (k2tog)3 times, knit 1**.

Repeat from * to** to last 18 sts. Finish: knit 1, (k2tog)3 times, (make 1, knit 1)2 times, make 1, (k2tog)3 times, knit 3.

(106 sts)

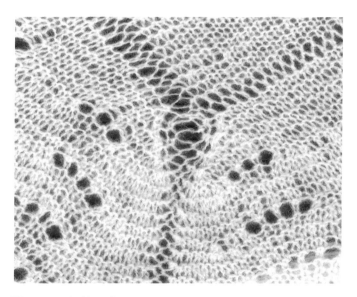

Row 74: Knit to last 2 sts, k2tog.   **(105 sts)**

Row 75: K2tog., knit to last 2 sts, k2tog.   **(103 sts)**

Row 76: K2tog., knit to last 2 sts, k2tog.   **(101 sts)**

Row 77: K2tog., knit to last 2 sts, k2tog.   **(99 sts)**

Row 78: K2tog., knit to last 2 sts, k2tog.   **(97 sts)**

Row 79: K2tog., knit to last 2 sts, k2tog.   **(95 sts)**

Row 80: K2tog., knit to last 2 sts, k2tog.   **(93 sts)**

Row 81: K2tog., knit to last 2 sts, k2tog.   **(91 sts)**

Make four borders exactly the same leaving the 'loops' (meaning the last row's 91 sts) on a thread each for three of the borders.

With the 4th border, continue knitting the centre square in the following way:

The top and sides of the centre square are <u>mattress stitched</u> to the stitches in the borders. This is done by using a length of wool and running it loosely and evenly through each stitch/side loop in turn, see detail above. The borders are also mattress stitched to the lace edges. See pictures next page.

Rows 82 & 83 *Break Pattern Rows* both the same: Knit 1, (make 1, k2tog) to end **(91 sts).** See arrowed photo next page. For garter stitch centre, simply continue to knit rows on 4th border for "double the number of stitches" so (2 x 91) = 182 rows. *Mattress Stitch* the sides and top border onto the centre, and again Mattress Stitch the borders up to their edgings, then <u>closely sew</u> together the edgings so that they appear as a complete corner point. Sew in all ends and dress the shawl.

Note: If you want to use one of the "72 Row" colour recipes on pages 31 – 39, or for the Morag Shawl page 27, with these directions you can: Simply follow directions for this shawl till Border Row 2 is done, then put in 4 plain rows first before following your chosen chart from Row 1, so that the recipe's "Row 3" pattern row matches up with this one's "Row 9".   Still do shapings as shown on Hap Border Chart as you change colours per recipe. I've put the Row Strip at the side of the border chart to help do this, page 18.   When the Colour chart's 72 rows are done, resume these directions for Rows 79 – 83.

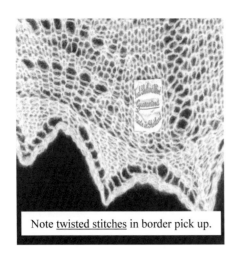

Note twisted stitches in border pick up.

Left :

This hap has a "quality control" label machine-sewn onto it to show it has passed inspection, it says *Real Shetland Wool <u>Guaranteed</u> Made in Shetland*. A system of labelling like this dates back to 1927 (W.P. Livingstone).

Below:

An undressed sample of this exact hap pattern worked in the colourway shown on page 38, using Jamieson's Shetland Ultra 2 ply and a 3mm needle. This would dress to make a lovely shoulder shawl of c 36 inches / 90 cm. A larger shawl would be got by using a larger needle and / or thicker yarn. Quantities must be estimated by knitter – buy in plenty, remember, you can always use up oddments in swatches, granny square afghans, or donate your oddments to children or new knitters, so that they learn to knit with good yarn!

If you decide to knit in colours, all ends must be woven in invisibly. Then, with a length of main colour (the same as edging and centre) border sides should be sewn together; it might be an idea to lace the borders together more tightly for a continuous effect. Both "mattress stitching" and "close lacing" were used in the borders of the originals, as you will see from the photographs in this book.

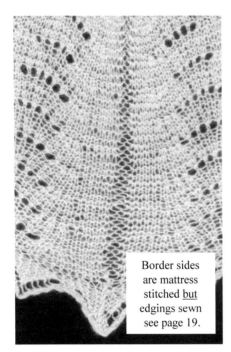

Border sides are mattress stitched <u>but</u> edgings sewn see page 19.

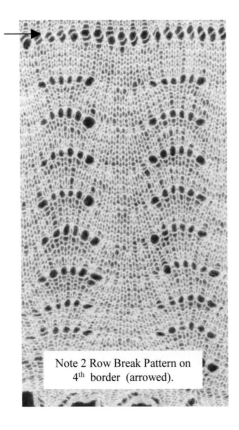

Note 2 Row Break Pattern on 4th border (arrowed).

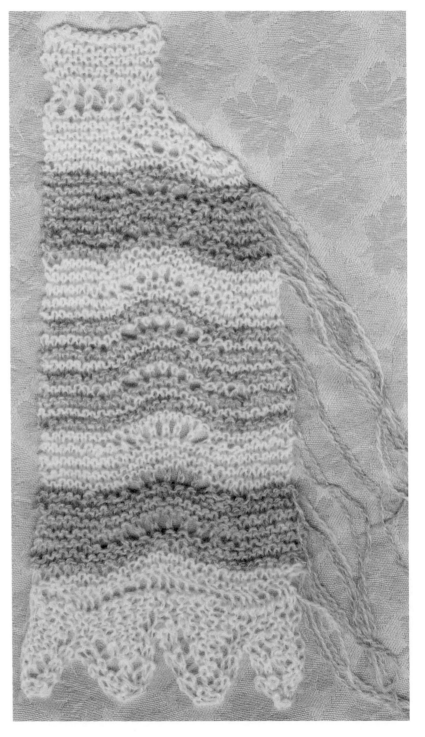

Hap Shawl: Second Traditional Method ("Borders Inwards")

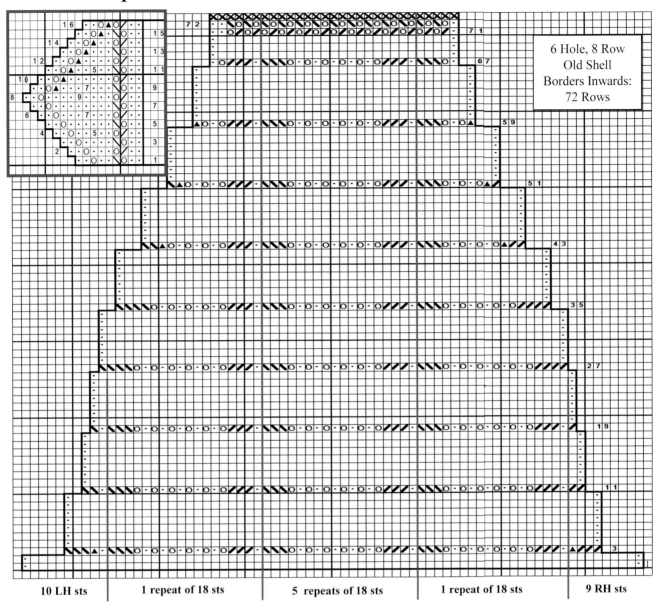

6 Hole, 8 Row
Old Shell
Borders Inwards:
72 Rows

| 10 LH sts | 1 repeat of 18 sts | 5 repeats of 18 sts | 1 repeat of 18 sts | 9 RH sts |

I give this second time-honoured method for purists. The chart is closely based on one for a "Scalloped Shawl" in a *Bestway* brochure dated c1955. It's interesting to compare this method with the hap pattern chart on page 18; particularly to see how the first 5 stitches of each border side are decreased immediately on Row 3; this is done to give fullness to the edging strip at the corners. I made a 'crepe' shawl in this manner once, but must admit I didn't enjoy the border matching and centre grafting it involved - that may have been because I was making it in a fine yarn which meant a lot more stitches and rows than this one involves. The border chart above, is taken from a traditional pattern that used a 4 ply wool and UK 5 / 5.5 mm / US 8 or 9 needle. **To make a shawl in this manner:** follow the Triangular Lace Edging Chart (inset) and make 12 points. Pick up **145 sts** from straight side of edging: 12 per point + 1. (For all four borders = 48 points: the stitch total is 145 x 4 = **580 sts**.) Knit next row and then divide knitting to match chart for Row 1 by marking into sections to show:

10 LH sts + 18 + (5 x 18 = 90) + 18 + 9 RH sts = 145 stitches per border.

Now, knit pattern as above chart for each border, changing colours if required by following selected colourway from your choice of colour chart. Note: **If you make all four borders at once by 'knitting in the round' purl even border rows. After Row 72**, cast off (as written then and charted here) 101 stitches: (5 x 18 = 90 + 6 LH + 5 RH sts) OR better, reserve these stitches for centre*. The 1950s pattern's "cast off stitches version" then directed the knitter to make 3 more matching borders (*herring bone laced* together) and sew these to a previously made separately knitted centre square that was 96 sts wide by 168 rows high. The next directions were to make and sew on four edging strips! The original Shetland knitters famously didn't do this "casting off + sewing up" method: that pattern had been "Anglicised" by the pattern commissioners; meaning the directions were deliberately simplified for English knitters, who supposedly weren't familiar - or obviously weren't considered proficient enough to manage the Shetland technique.

* **Alternatively, if you reserved the border stitches as I suggest, you can sew the border flaps together to make an empty square. Then, by using 101 sts from a border, knit up a centre square 202 rows high – this larger number means you can more easily attach it to the two vertical sides' reserved sts (by knitting the last stitch of each centre row "2 tog" with a side border stitch in turn). Graft the final 101 sts to the last border's 101 sts. Sew in all ends and dress.**

Returning from the Market

Both these early 1900s postcards record Shetland women walking and knitting with shawls pulled up over their heads. In the photo above, the first knitter is wearing 'rivlins' – hide shoes. The shawl border of the second knitter which can be seen clearly, I have recorded in Collection 6. Their Shetland ponies are loaded with packages in 'kishies' (rush baskets) lashed to their sides.

"Knitting is the grand employment of all classes of females, high and low. The better classes display their taste in shawls and scarfs *(sic)* of every variety of pattern, shape and colour; and the humbler classes confine themselves to stockings, gloves and cravats. They are never idle. You see the lower orders busy knitting when footing their way through the marshes with creels on their backs."

Notes on a Tour of Shetland and Orkney, D Sutherland, 1846. Perhaps the "scarfs" are what we'd term small stoles now.

Rivlins can be seen again in this second contemporarily coloured view, as too can kishies, here carrying peat, the local abundant fuel, as wood was rare in these "treeless" islands. Both walkers are knitting, the one on the left is working a long stocking.   Note how the facing knitter carries her ball of wool in her apron pocket. She may even be knitting a hap edging strip, as that appears to be what is hanging from under her left arm. The haps worn here are single coloured in what is shown as brown and grey.

Shetlanders

Hap Shawl: Modern Method ("Borders Outwards")

The following method is sometimes referred to as "English" or "Victorian Shetland". One of the earliest photographed shawls showing this exact method that I've seen is of one worn by Kate Steel of The Hebrides in 1954 (Paul Strand Archive Foundation, pictured in *Traditional Knitted Lace Shawls*, Martha Waterman, Interweave Press 1998). Her shawl is shown with a <u>diamond</u> centre, its borders picked up and "knitted in the round" (using corner stitches with 'make ones' each side for increases) then has the Traditional Peaked Edging (see page 43) used to complete. That may have been done on a circular needle as these were developed in the 1920s/40s; but it could equally have been knitted using a set of double pointed needles. You can either knit in the round with a corner stitch (2a) – I show this experienced knitter's method for the **Morag Shawl** – or, for an easier method (2b) you can "flat knit" each border flap. To start with for either method, you need a **diamond centre** (by this I mean a diagonally knitted square).

1 Diamond Centre see page 28 : Cast on 1 st. Increase (a stitch for every row) by "**wrapping wool round needle, knit to last stitch: knit into <u>back</u> of last st**" **each** row; till you have **170 sts**. Then, decrease a stitch a row ("**wool round needle, slip 1, k2tog, p.s.s.o., knit to last stitch: knit into back of last st**") till 2 stitches are left: k2tog., = 1 st again. You should have 85 stitch loops down each side. (Maths check: 170 divided by 2 = 85). If you want a **square centre**: With Knitting Cast on (page 62) cast on 85 sts and knit for 170 rows.

Now read and follow directions for either 2a or 2b for how to knit the borders.

2a For "*knitting in the round*" - Expert's method:
Pick up all round 85 sts per side - <u>at the same time</u>: increase into every 5th st by 'knitting and purling' into it = 102 sts per side. (Maths check : 85 divided by 5 = 17, so you actually add 17 to 85 to get 102 sts per side). Mark the knitting up so that it has **101 border + 1 corner st per side** x 4. Knit next row and then divide and mark knitting for each border, this time to match Chart 1, next page, for Row 1 - <u>additionally</u> marking into sections to show:

6 LH sts + (5 x 18 = 90) + 5 RH sts + 1 corner stitch (starred on chart) = 102 stitches per border.

<u>Set Up Pattern Rows</u>: As shown by the 4 rows beneath the green line of Chart 1's Row 1, page 24. (These give the lacy pattern near the centre to mimic the lacy Rows 71 and 72 of the "Borders Inwards" method, see page 21.) Now work the rows as shown by Charts 1 & 2, page 24, changing colours to match your chosen colour chart, **purl all even rounds**.

Stitches per border after Row 72: 168 sts. (7 x 18 sts = 126) + 21 LH and 20 RH sts + 1 corner stitch.
Row 73 a decreasing row: Knit 4, "knit 2, K2tog" 40 times, knit 4 = **128 sts.** (Maths check: 168 – 8 side sts = 160sts. 160 -40 = 120. 120 + 8 side sts = 128.) Work edging as charted on this page round each border, using up 8 border sts per edging's 16 rows – 16 complete points. If substituting a different edging, it might be an idea to adjust your decreasing row a bit to suit your chosen edging; for example, If using an edging with 12 rows, decrease evenly so each border has 132 sts (11 x 12) and you'll have 22 complete points a side - as you'll use up 6 border sts per point.

2b To "*flat knit*" each border separately*: Pick up 85 sts per side, at the same time: increase into every 5th stitch by 'knitting and purling' into it until last stitch: knit final stitch = **101 sts per side**. (Maths check : 80 divided by 5 = 16; so you will actually add 16 sts to 85 to get 101 sts per side.) Knit next row and then divide knitting to match chart 1 on page 25 for Row 1, by marking into sections to show:

6 LH sts + (5 x 18 = 90) + 5 RH sts = 101 stitches per border.

Now pattern as charted there for each border side, work the 4 Set Up Border Pattern Rows first (below green line) these give the lacy pattern near the centre to mimic the lacy Rows 71 and 72 of "Borders Inwards" method. **Then follow pattern rows from Row 1. Change colours if required by following selected colour banding from colourway charts.**
Stitches per border after Row 72: 167 sts (7 x 18 sts = 126) + 21 LH and 20 RH sts. **Row 73** (decreasing row): knit 6, 'knit 2 knit 2 tog' 39 times, knit 5 = **128 sts.** You can now join borders by sewing or *herringbone lacing* (page 13) or you can knit the edging shown here across each border flap before sewing them.

3 Edging – either method: Cast on 8 stitches with Knitting Cast On. Knit RH edging as shown here, across border(s) at rate of 16 points per border. (This means that odd numbered rows are knitted on the reverse side of the shawl, even numbered rows are on the front.) At the end of every even row, cast off the next border stitch in turn by knitting it "2 tog through back of loops" with the final edging row stitch: 8 sts used up per point for 16 points (Maths check: 128 divided by 8 = 16) Shown as final "\" on charted even rows. Note, no corner gathering is needed for this narrow edging. After edging is completed, sew in all ends and dress shawl as page 49.

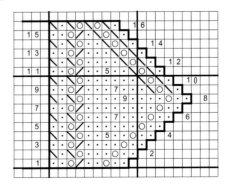

*see Note **under this method's Chart 1, page 25, about making all 4 borders at once.**

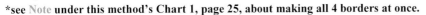

Hap Border – "Borders Outwards"
Method 2a : Knitting in the Round
- Do bottom Chart 1 first, see page 23. Purl all even rounds!

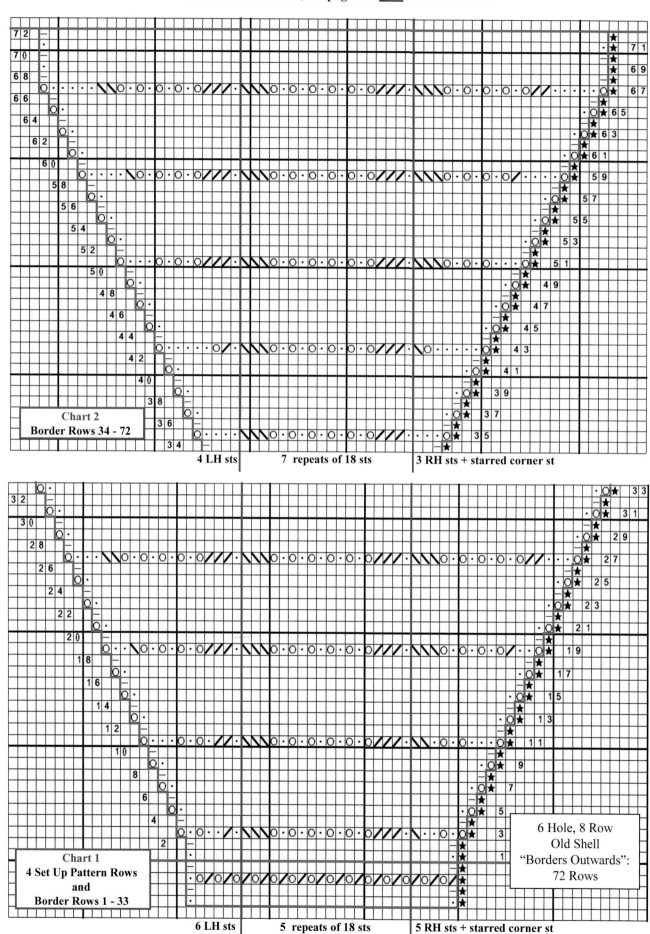

Chart 2
Border Rows 34 - 72

4 LH sts   7 repeats of 18 sts   3 RH sts + starred corner st

Chart 1
4 Set Up Pattern Rows
and
Border Rows 1 - 33

6 Hole, 8 Row
Old Shell
"Borders Outwards":
72 Rows

6 LH sts   5 repeats of 18 sts   5 RH sts + starred corner st

Hap Border – "Borders Outwards"
Method 2b : Flat Knitting
- Do bottom **Chart 1** first, see page 23. <u>Knit</u> all even rows!

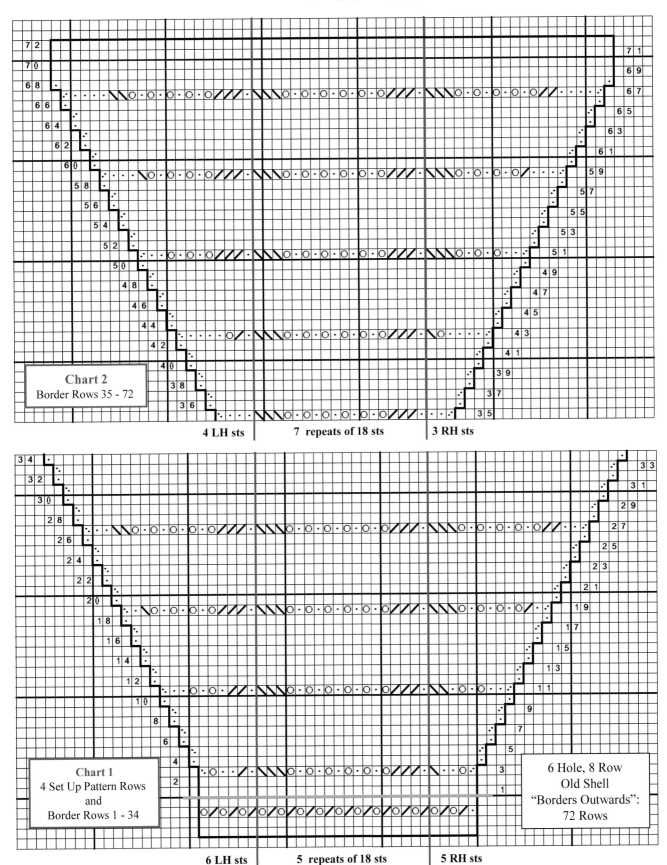

Chart 2
Border Rows 35 - 72

4 LH sts | 7 repeats of 18 sts | 3 RH sts

Chart 1
4 Set Up Pattern Rows
and
Border Rows 1 - 34

6 Hole, 8 Row
Old Shell
"Borders Outwards":
72 Rows

6 LH sts | 5 repeats of 18 sts | 5 RH sts

"Set Up Pattern Rows" shown below green horizontal line on Chart 1.

Note: You can pick up and flat knit all 4 borders at once, using a circular needle. This would mean that you have only one seam – when you have done all four borders "Row 1s", <u>turn the knitting</u> and do all the four "Row 2s"; keep turning the knitting for every new charted row, see page 13, which shows position of final seam as a red dotted line on diagram, top right.

The Morag Shawl

This traditional shawl is made closely in keeping with the style and shading of an original Shetland hap in that it is made in a *jumper weight* range of undyed Shetland wool colours, quantities and colours listed on next page. This wool is the nearest most of us will get to working with yarns similar to the hand spun worsted used in the 1880s for these practical warm shawls. The pattern itself is a deliberate recreation of a Victorian hap, but my shawl differs from true Shetland pieces in that it is knitted "Borders Outwards", and with a diagonal knitted centre (described as "English" or "Victorian Shetland"), see method **2a**, page 23. The large triangular edging is the one shown on that page.

I give this shawl to show you how to use a chart + border colour design to create a hap. You could use any of the border colour recipes given on pages 31 – 39 instead, or simply try another edging with this one – see page 43, for some ideas. Better still, you can create your own 72 row coloured design to use – photocopy off the chart you want and colour in the rows as you'd like or make your own recipe strip (see page 49 for template). Experienced knitters can readily adapt the pattern for a thoroughly authentic square centred shawl made to the "Borders Inward" method and chart, page 21.

Circular Needle:

UK 8 / 4.00mm / US 6 : 60cm / 24inches long

Dressed Tension over Centre:

16 sts x 24 rows = 10cm / 4 inches

Finished Dressed Size:

54 inches / 135cm square.

"Err...this wool smells irresistible - forgive me?" Caught red handed! One year old Suki was so impressed with this shawl she settled to sleep on it as it dried on dressing wires and so was photographed. Luckily, she is an obedient cat and was easily trained when a kitten not to attack wool, but sometimes a shawl is obviously just what a girl cat needs too! For details of how to dress a shawl, see page 49.

An alternative hap edging is shown below left, though you can choose any edging you think appropriate instead.

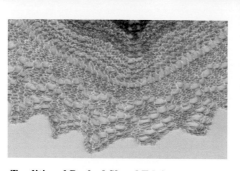

Traditional Peaked Shawl Edging, page 43.

Morag Shawl Colours

Yarn Quantities and Colours

For a single colour (one colour) shawl, the jumper weight yarn required would be just under 450g of a colour. If you preferred the lighter Shetland *lace weight*, it would need around 250g of a single colour with the same needle. **Please Note**: If you intend to substitute, allow for at least 10% extra of each colour yarn to allow for tension differences, slight changes of design etc. To give you a guide for comparison: if you start with making the centre, this took approx 125g of main colour jumper weight. **For two easier "Borders Inwards" methods, see pages 18 and 21.**

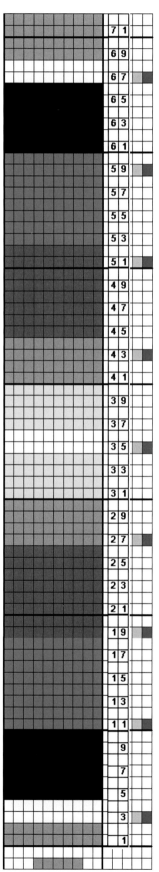

The Morag Shawl's *jumper weight** quantities are as follows:

Main: 11 x 25g balls Brown shade 2007 (Sholmit) - actually used approx 270g

1 x 25g ball White shade 2001 - actually used approx 15g

2 x 25g balls Black shade 2005 - actually used approx 30g

3 x 25g balls Dark Grey shade 2009 (Yuglet) - actually used approx 60g

2 x 25g balls Red Brown shade 2004 (Moorit) - actually used approx 40g

1 x 25g ball Light Grey shade 2008 (Katmollet) - actually used approx 25g

*A feature of this natural yarn is the inclusion of quite wiry guard hairs, these can be easily pulled out if preferred.

I made my shawl following Modern Method 2a, ("Borders Outwards") page 24, and followed that pattern chart exactly, so I did my Break Pattern first as shown on that page's chart (but shown here on this "Inwards" chart right as Rows 71 and 72). I then changed for the border's colours at the start of the rounds as shown by the Colour Chart on this page; so, reading here from the bottom:

Rows 69 – 72 Brown - Importantly, for "Borders Outwards" methods - knit Rows 71 & 72 in plain garter stitch instead.

Rows 67 – 68 White - Row 67 is a pattern row

Rows 61 – 66 Black

Rows 53 – 60 Dark Grey - Row 59 is a pattern row

Rows 45 – 52 Red Brown - Row 51 is a pattern row

Rows 41 – 44 Brown - Row 43 is a pattern row

Rows 37 – 40 Light Grey

Rows 35 – 36 White - Row 35 is a pattern row

Rows 31 – 34 Light Grey

Rows 27 – 30 Brown - Row 27 is a pattern row

Rows 19 – 26 Red Brown - Row 19 is a pattern row

Rows 11 – 18 Dark Grey - Row 11 is a pattern row

Rows 5 – 10 Black

Rows 3 - 4 White - Row 3 is a pattern row – see note 1 below

Rows 1 – 2 Brown

After the 72 border rows, I did the decreasing* to get down to 128 sts per border then turned the knitting "inside out" (see next page) and knitted the edging* round the shawl.

Notes :

1. Old Shell Lace Pattern Rows are shown here by orange/blue squares on the RH side of this chart, and correspond with Pattern Charts shown on page 24.

2. The "yellow squares" (by Rows 71 - 72) show the Break Pattern Rows for a top of border near the centre, and are for knitting an "Inwards" method only – page 21.

3. Brown squares shown here below Row 1, show the shawl's centre square and edging colour ("main colour").

*Read directions for this on page 23.

Tips for 'Knitting in the Round' and Diamond Centres see page 23

Right: A **"flat knitted"** diamond centre for a lace hap made in Shetland Cobweb 1 ply and a UK 13 /2.25mm / US 0 or 1 needle. In this case, the centre's been knitted as a diamond centre "square". A pink stitch marker - circled, approximately halfway down the right-hand side, shows that this is the front or "odd row side" upwards; if I'd been knitting an even row this would automatically be on the left-hand side as the knitting is turned.

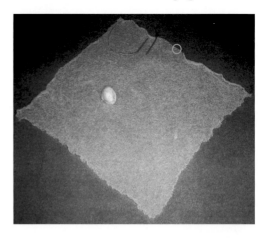

Diamond Centres are used because they can look better when worn as then the centre part's garter stitch rows run straight across from shoulder to shoulder instead of diagonally as they'll appear with a folded Square knit centre. Diamond Centres weren't traditional in Shetland Haps, but were part used as triangles for 'point shawls' or 'half haps' - page 41.

Note for the "Borders Outwards" methods: where stitches are picked up round the centre's sides and the border is "knitted in the round"- outwards, see photograph, left. See how I have marked the corners with stitch markers and a contrast thread of black yarn to identify them. The start of a round is marked with the large blue stitch marker, the black thread opposite marks the opposite corner - the halfway point; and the two small pink stitch markers show the other two corners; I'm working an Old Shell lace hap border. As the knitting is done these markers can be moved upwards on the same corner stitch column. I always think this looks rather like you are knitting a bag, and handily, you can drop your ball of yarn into it between sessions! **Tip:** Once shawl borders are completely knitted, turn the knitting "bag" inside out by pushing the knitting through the "round" of the needle - you do this to keep the odd rows (pattern rows) of the edging and the borders on the same face / side of the shawl. It's a nice thing for purists, but not essential!

This postcard *Dressing Hap Shawls* is c 1905, and from it we can tell there are many shawls dressed in layers on each frame; so many, that in the foreground there are two stretchers separated by a wooden pole, with single coloured (plain) shawls set to dry. All around are other loaded stretchers - interestingly, these all have a top layer of light haps with darker colour bands. It's hard to be certain, but there appears to be about 13/14 edging points per side. On this same postcard 1905, a rather scary paternal direction was sent from Lerwick to Kent : *Dear Florrie, I am sending you this card – has a pattern for you to make a shawl by. You will see how the Shetland ladies are dressing their shawls, you must try and make one for yourself. I hope you are doing well at school. Father.* Poor Florrie seems to have a lot to live up to for a schoolgirl!

Hap Border Colours Collection

This Shetland knitter stands somewhat nervously outside a croft, one bright blustery day for a photograph which it appears she wasn't expecting to be taken. She wears an old undressed dark "Borders Inwards" hap but appears to be knitting a hap "Outwards". This press photograph taken in the 1930s, shows how practical country fashions in dress lingered on in Shetland for at least 70 years. Only the shorter skirt is a concession to its decade; otherwise, this knitter wouldn't have looked out of place in 1860.

How to change the size of a "Borders Outwards" Shawl
for a 6 Hole, 4 Row version of an Old Shell Border, as charted below.

A 6 Hole, 4 Row Old Shell "outwards" border. Chart, page 39.

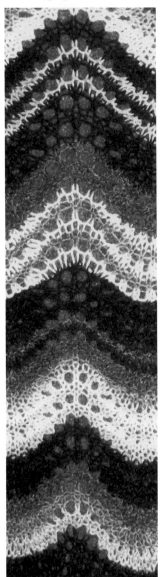

One must be certain of overall finished size before starting a "Borders Inwards" shawl as it's only by a radical decreasing in the border pattern that one can reduce its finished size. Changing for "outwards" shawls is easier, and there are 3 ways to enlarge/reduce the size of an "Outwards" shawl. **1.** Make the border longer or shorter. **2.** Change the centre size to start with. **3.** Put a wider edging on, or put in an insertion as the knitter did with the wide 3 Hole Edging, shown page 10. These ways are explained in more detail next.

1. The border can be made as deep as wanted, **just repeat Chart Rows 1 – 36 shown below** until you get to a depth you want to finish on. Then knit 4 rows plain and a decrease row of 'k2, k2tog' (to get rid of ¼ of the sts) before you work your edging.

2. Another good way of changing the overall finished size of a shawl is to alter the actual size of the centre; for the chart on this page, simply keep to the following formula:

Cast on **X** multiples of 18 + (2 + 3 = 5 side stitches).

e.g. I'd use **5** "multiples of 18" + (5 side stitches) to get the **cast on 95 + 1 corner stitch = 96 sts (square)** or for a diamond shaped centre instead, the maximum **"stitches per row" before decreasing would be 96 x 2 = 192 sts – see page 23.**

8 or **10** "multiples of 18" may be used if a larger shawl is wanted, or for one with finer wool: e.g. Cast on **10** x 18 + (5 side stitches) = 185 sts for a **square** centre, and work for 2 x 185 = 370 rows.

If a **Diamond Centre** (page 23) is wanted or a **triangle for a half hap shawl** (page 41) the calculation still applies, but this time the maximum stitch count of the triangle will be **twice** the total e.g. 185 **x 2** = 370 stitches. So, you would cast on a stitch, increase each row until there are 370 stitches in the triangle. Then, if you wanted a diamond "centre square", you'd complete by decreasing to 1 stitch again; following the advice given for the Diamond Centre, page 23. You should have 185 laceholes to pick up into per side.

3. Chose a wider edging or put in an insertion before your edging, see *Heirloom Knitting.*

> **Quantities Note:** I'm sorry but it's not possible to give exact quantities for each of the shawls' colourways on pages 31 to 39 as it will depend on so many factors: needle size, overall size, tension/gauge, yarn used; so my advice is please allow for plenty of each colour and if possible, *please* use Shetland wool for the best and most authentic results.
>
> **Extra yarn always comes in useful** (for later swatching, making granny square blankets) or you can even give the leftovers to aspiring knitters so they can work with good yarn!

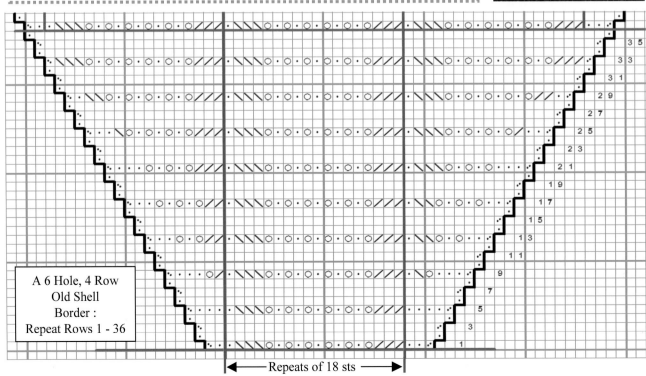

A 6 Hole, 4 Row Old Shell Border : Repeat Rows 1 - 36

← Repeats of 18 sts →

Hap Traditional Colours Collection 1

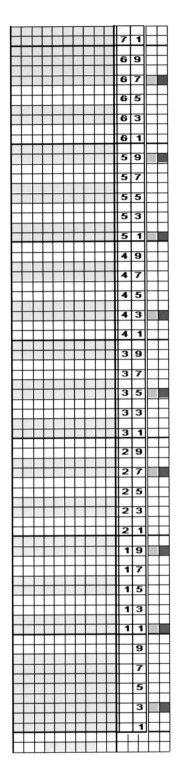
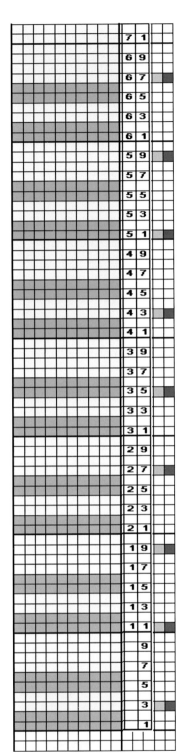
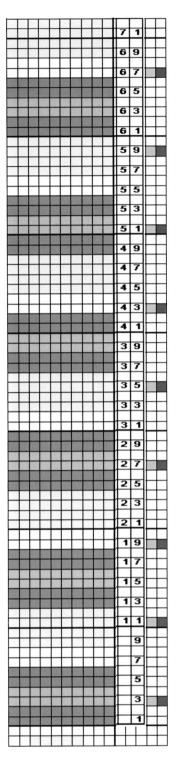

Left Pattern: The simplest of shading patterns, this "piping stripes" one is taken from 1900s haps - centre background of the *Dressing Shetland Shawls* photograph (cover) and from page 12. Similar shawls are white with (other single colour) narrowly spaced stripes; or conversely, single coloured with white stripes: e.g. a brown hap with white stripes. **Centre and Right Patterns:** Inspired by a 1940s brochure. The hap offered in this was baby blue with mid blue and yellow stripes (centre); it was easy to use this as an inspiration and design a "3 pinks and white" alternative (shown right, with palest, light and mid pink – the palest pink being the main colour); a "3 blues and white" one could be easily created instead.

Each shawl's main colour is given below the first row so, for example, the Centre shawl's main colour for centre and edging is **light blue**; the border's bands (three colours) are of **mid blue** (e.g.1 – 2 & 5 - 6); **primrose** (3 – 4); **light blue** (7 – 10). It might be better if the bandings were doubled for a "fewer stripes" version : e.g. Rows 1 - 4 mid blue, 4 - 8 primrose, 9 - 12 mid blue. 13 - 20 pale blue, etc. If you are knitting Borders Outwards, consider first if your chart's colours need working "top down" to keep the colours in the correct position on the border: e.g. start the RH chart's colouring with 4 pink rows, then 2 white, and so on. **Rows 3, 11, 19, 27, 35, 43, 51, 59, 67 and 71-72 are "Inwards" pattern rows, page 21.**

Hap Traditional Colours Collection 2

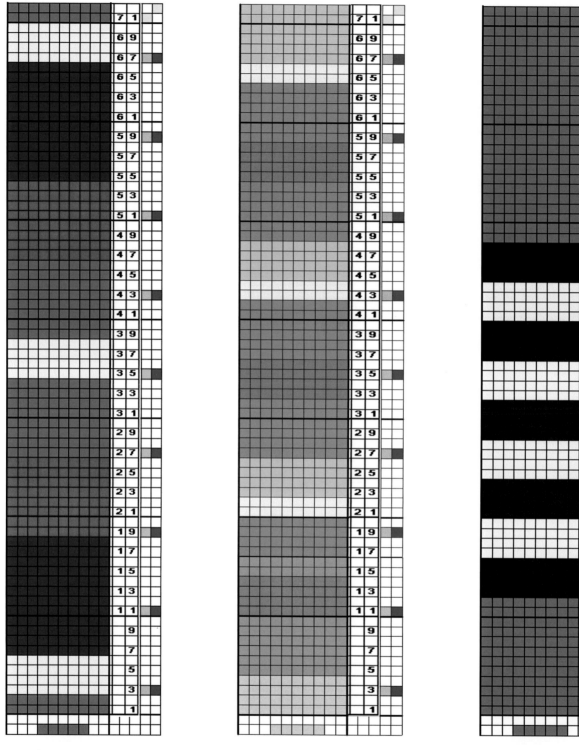

Left, Centre and Right Patterns: These wide, regularly striped border designs are taken from 1880s onwards grey haps. A feature shared by most of these early ones I've seen is symmetrically reflective banding, by this I mean colours that shade to a centre colour (e.g. white, Row 36 for Left Pattern) and then sequence out again. This is also demonstrated in the Right Pattern, the midway stripe for this being deep red. The centre pattern has a traditional repeating waves-of-colour design. Again, as always, colour-ways can be switched to suit your taste for any of these "recipes".

Each shawl's main colour is given below the first row so, for example, the Left shawl's main colour for centre and edging is **mid grey**; the border's bands (four colours) are of **mid grey** (e.g. 1 – 2); **white** (3 – 6); **dark grey** (7 – 18); and a **madder red** (19 – 26). Madder is a scarlet dye that is made from a plant, deep crimson or blue may be less "loud" colours!

If you are knitting Borders Outwards, always consider first if your chart's colours need working "top down" to keep the colours in the correct position on the border. For example, you'd start the RH chart's colouring with 24 grey rows, and so on. **Rows 3, 11, 19, 27, 35, 43, 51, 59, 67 and 71 - 72 are "Inwards" pattern rows - see chart, page 21.**

Hap Traditional Colours Collection 3

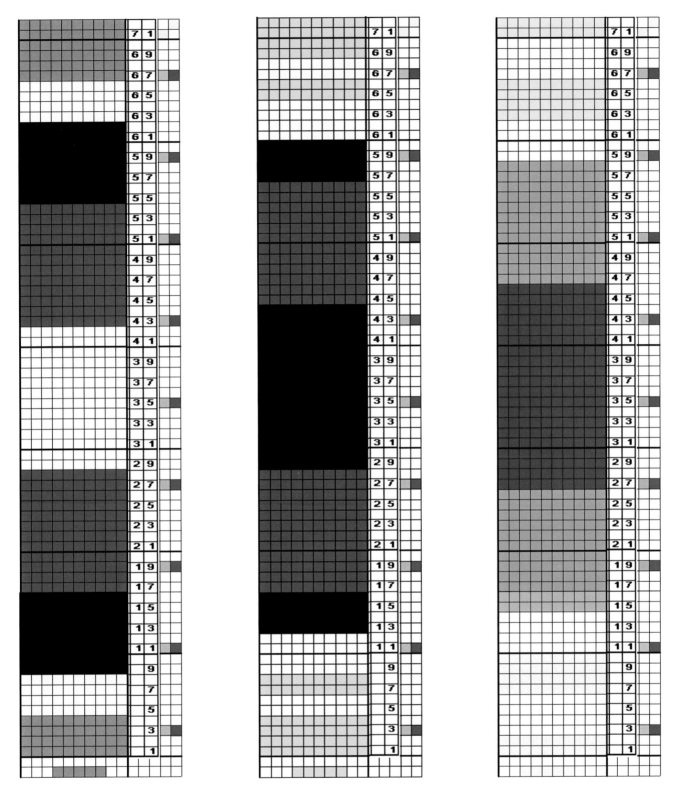

Left, Centre and Right Patterns: These regular wider striped designs are taken from early haps. The centre patterning is taken from the *Dressing Shetland Shawls,* frontispiece, the girl kneeling is looking at one like this. I have made the centre one here have narrow dark stripes (Rows 13 – 16, Rows 57 - 60). Lighter shades - pinks - could be used instead, as I've shown with the Right design.

Each shawl's main colour is given below the first row so, for example, the Left shawl's main colour for centre and edging is **mid brown**; the border's bands (four colours) are of **mid-brown or Shetland mogit** (e.g. 1 – 4); **white** (5 – 8); **black** (9 – 16); and a **red-brown or Shetland moorit** (17 – 28). Obviously, as all these traditional designs are symmetrically reflective, you'll get a pretty similar result if you knitted these either the Borders Outwards or Borders Inwards methods.

Rows 3, 11, 19, 27, 35, 43, 51, 59, 67and 71-72 are "Inwards" pattern rows - see chart, page 21.

Hap Traditional Colours Collection 4

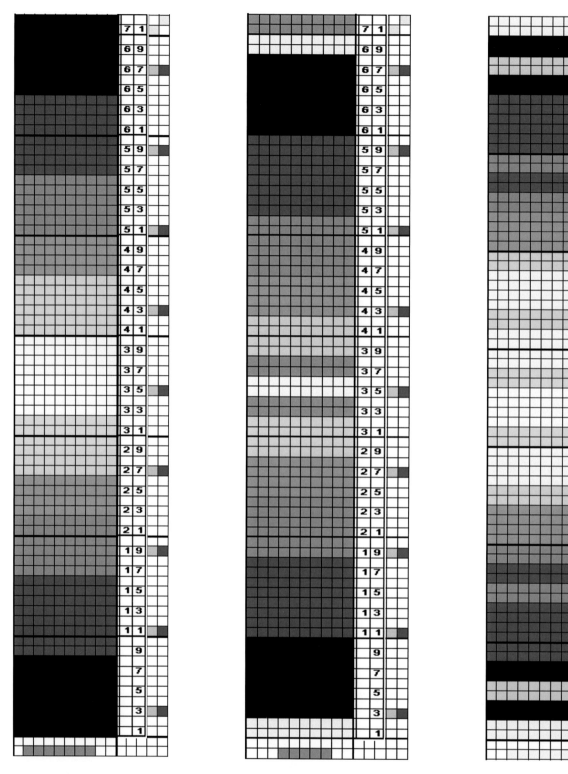

Left, Centre and Right Patterns: These regular spaced border designs and the ones following are all taken from 1880s+ black and white photographs that give no true indication of colour. However, shadings are clearly apparent, so the patterns I give from here on use the natural colours of the fleeces to replicate these as far as possible. Knitters can easily substitute their own colours. **Note:** the Right pattern of a white hap is <u>2 rows longer</u> than the others. Each shawl's main colour is given below the first row in each case so, for example, the Left shawl's main colour for centre and edging is **light brown**; the border's bands (six colours) are of **black** (e.g.1 – 8); **red-brown** (9 – 16); **brown** (17 – 22); and a **mid-brown** (23 – 26); **grey** (27 – 32): **white** (33 – 40). In Shetland colours these could be: black, moorit, mooskit (or mogit), gaulmogot (or eesit), shaela (or sholmit) and natural white; the main colour being gaulmogot/eesit, see page 14.

If you are knitting Borders Outwards, consider if your chart's colours need working "top down" to keep the colours in the correct position on the border: e.g. you'd start the middle chart's colouring with 2 brown rows, and so on. **Rows 3, 11, 19, 27, 35, 43, 51, 59, 67 and 71 - 72 are "Inwards" pattern rows - see chart, page 21.**

Hap Traditional Colours Collection 5

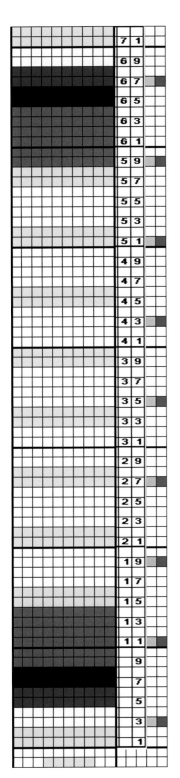
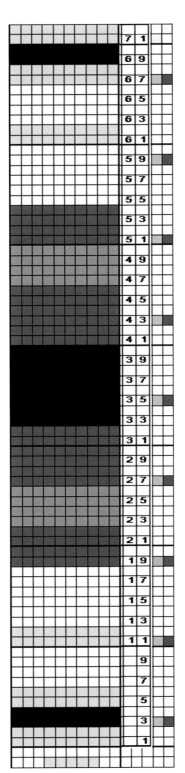
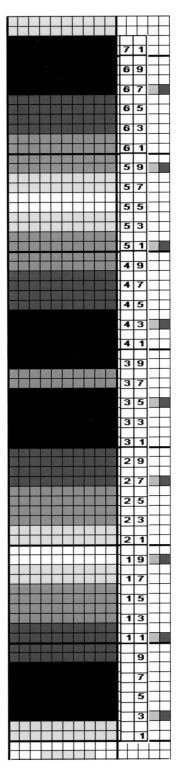

Left, Centre and Right Patterns: The Left pattern is taken from one shown in the background of the *Dressing Shetland Shawls* photograph, frontispiece, extreme right (behind lady dresser), which is very similar to that of 40 years later directly below it, in the photograph underneath. Knitters can substitute their own colours. Note, the pattern of the Right hap design is 2 rows longer than the others, so the Break Pattern is on Rows 73 – 74 as shown by the yellow squares at the chart's side.

Each shawl's main colour is given below the first row in each example, so all these shawls' main colour for centre and edging is **light/mid grey**. For the Left shawl, the border's bands (five colours) are of **light/mid grey** (e.g.1 – 2); **white** (3 – 4); **dark grey** (5 – 6) **black** (7 – 8); and a **mid brown** (9 – 14).

Obviously, as all these traditional designs are symmetrically reflective, you'll get a pretty similar result if you knitted these either by the Borders Outwards or Borders Inwards methods. **Rows 3, 11, 19, 27, 35, 43, 51, 59, 67 and 71-72 are "Inwards" pattern rows - see chart, page 21.**

Hap Traditional Colours Collection 6

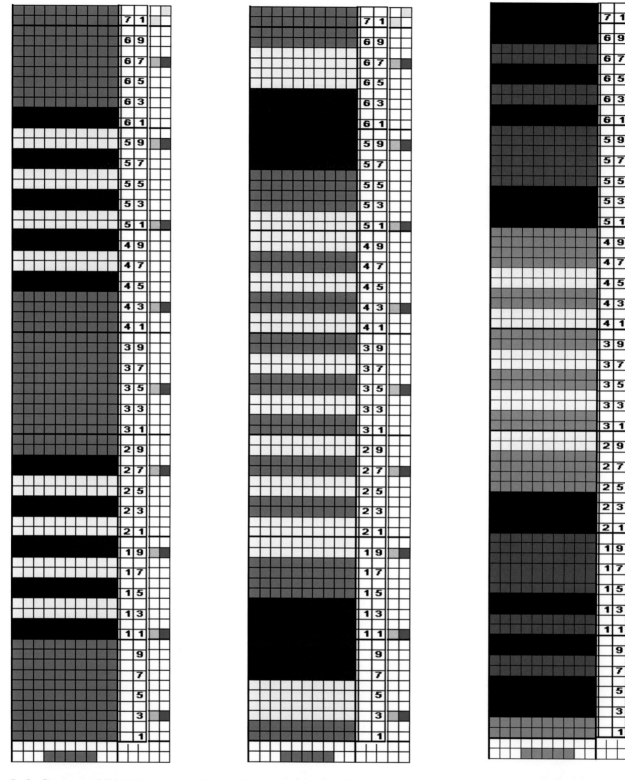

Left, Centre and Right Patterns: These wide, regularly striped border designs are taken from 1880s+ photographed haps. Again, change colours to suit if preferred. Left hap pattern is shown worn by the knitter in the *Returning from Market* photograph, page 22. The one on the right is taken from the *Washing and Dressing Shetland Shawls* photograph, page 9. The centre one is an alternative.

Each shawl's main colour is given below the first row so, for example, the Left shawl's main colour for centre and edging is **mid grey**; the border's bands (three colours) are of **mid grey** (e.g.1 – 10); **darkest red** (11 – 12); and a **white** (13 – 14).

If you are knitting "Borders Outwards", consider if your chart's colours need working "top down" to keep the colours in the correct position on the border: e.g. you'd start the RH chart's colouring with 4 black rows, and so on. **Rows 3, 11, 19, 27, 35, 43, 51, 59, 67 and 71 - 72 are "Inwards" pattern rows - see chart, page 21.**

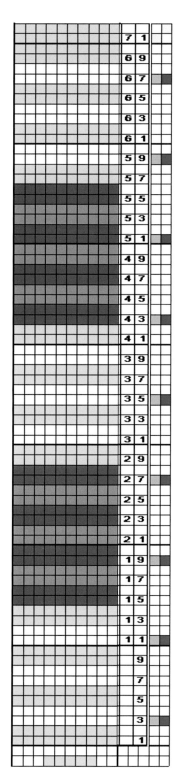
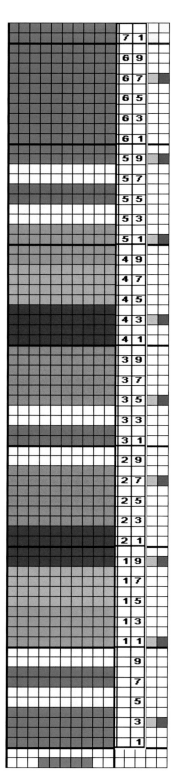
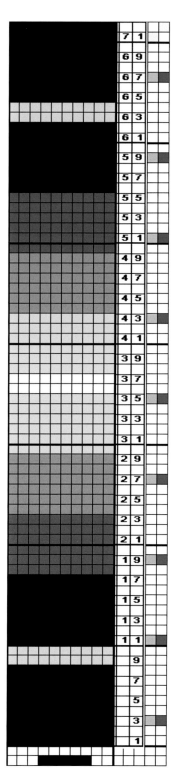

Left, Centre and Right Patterns: The Left pattern is from the centre background of the *Dressing Shetland Shawls* frontispiece, where the grey, or light brown shawl is stretched on a drying frame. White stripes are just detectable, I believe the darker bands would have been similarly shaded in two colours, and show it as such here. The last two designs I composed: the middle one is in a flecked grey and has stripes of white, bright violet, white, light lavender, shell pink, dark lavender, and rose pink. Replacing the two pinks with light and mid blue with a bright blue instead of violet, would be equally striking.

Each shawl's main colour is given below the first row so for example, the Left shawl's main colour for centre and edging is **light grey**; the border's bands (four colours) are of **light grey** (e.g.1 – 2); **white** (3 – 4); **mid brown** (15 – 16); and a **light brown** (17 – 18). **Rows 3, 11, 19, 27, 35, 43, 51, 59, 67 and 71 - 72 are "Inwards" pattern rows - see chart, page 21.** If you are knitting Borders Outwards, consider if your chart's colours need working "top down" to keep the colours in the correct position on the border: e.g. you'd start the LH chart's colouring with <u>four</u> grey rows, then 2 white, and so on.

Hap Traditional Colours Collection 8

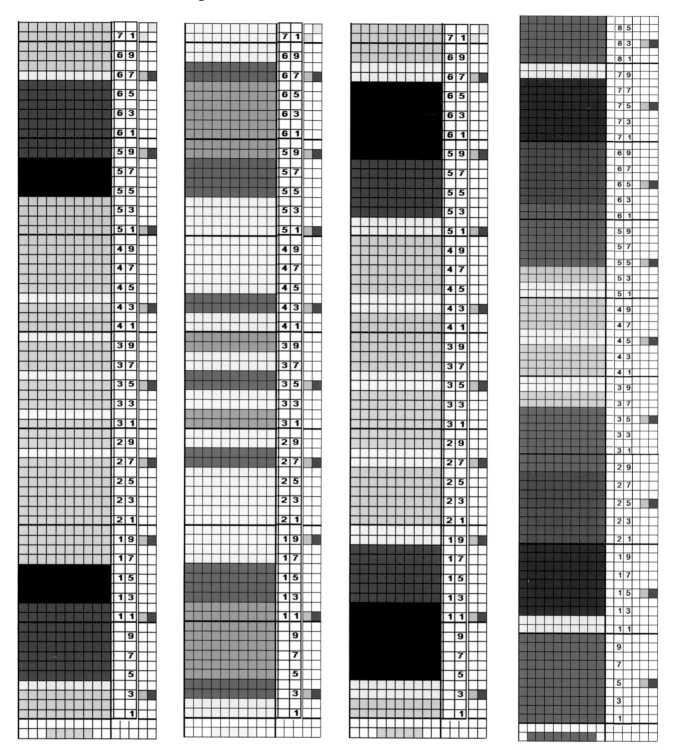

2 'Lefts', Centre and Right Patterns: This selection is based on a traditional "recipe" for hap colours (extreme left). The text said that the shawl would look equally good either all white, or with pink and blue – I give a colourway for this; the blues and pinks could be reversed or replaced with 2 shades of another colour. Interestingly, that pattern had single row colour bands (e.g. Left 1, Row 4). I prefer to work pairs of rows to keep colour changes on the back, and so show this with the pink/blue version. Having said all this, the photographed shawl was different to the written directions with that pattern! I give a similar one to that as the Third; which in turn is very like an 86 row-border hap in the Shetland Museum dating from before 1914. Interestingly, that is with a <u>10 row repeat</u> and has no Break Pattern (it had a large triangle edging of 16 points per side, and was an c.36 inches (92cm) square, I give this chart last. Its colours were: main - mottled grey, with bands of white, red-brown, mid-brown, dark and light grey. The borders were closely laced together and the hap was dressed more as a circle. Again, each shawl's main colour is given below the first row so, the Left's main colour for centre and edging is **light grey**; the border's bands (four colours) are of **light grey** (e.g. 1 – 3); **white** (4); **red-brown** (5 – 12); and a **black** (13 – 16). For the first <u>three</u> shawls **Rows 3, 11, 19, 27, 35, 43, 51, 59, 67 and 71 - 72 are "Inwards" pattern rows - see chart, page 21.** If you are knitting "Borders Outwards", consider if your chart's colours need working "top down" to keep the colours in the correct position on the border: e.g. you'd start the third chart's colouring with 4 grey rows, etc.

Hap Modern Colours

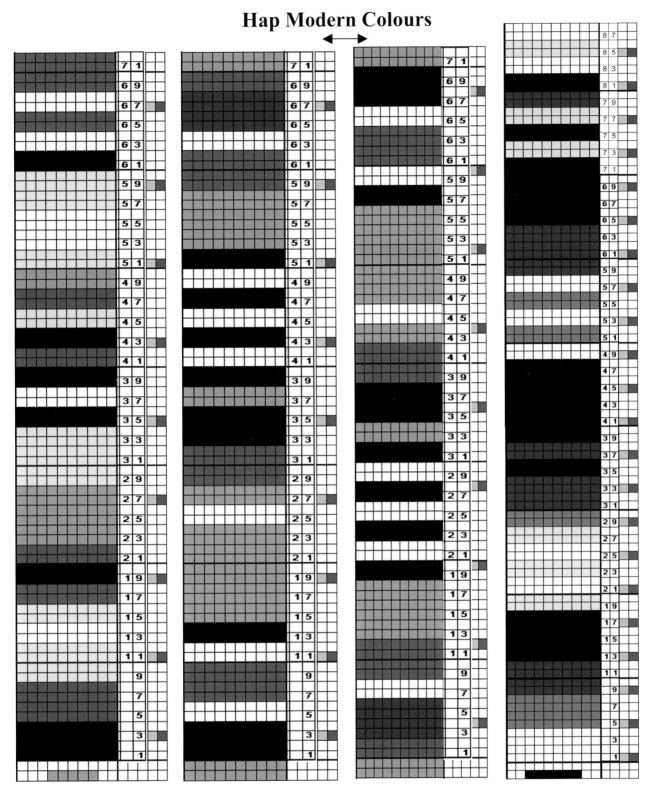

Left, 2 Centres and Right Patterns: Here are some ideas for "modern" random shadings for shawl borders. From the 1960s on, these busier asymmetric patterns became more common, and designing your own can be great fun. Obviously, these patternings differ from the previous ones as they <u>don't</u> reflect symmetrically; this should be considered when deciding which construction method to use – i.e. the traditional "Inwards" will put the black band of the second pattern's rows 1 – 4 at the hem of the shawl, the modern method "Outwards" will put it near the centre. So to correct this, for example, this design <u>flipped vertically</u> would look like the 3rd above – see arrow. The 4th pattern is for a 4 Row Old Shell, page 30, with a total of 88 rows. The others are '8 Row' ones, but could be '4' or '6 Row' ones instead. A 'browns' version is shown on front cover of this design.

Each shawl's main colour is given below the first row so, for example, the left shawl's main colour for centre and edging is **light brown**; the border's bands (five colours) are of **black** (e.g.1 – 4); **mid brown** (5 – 8); **grey** (9 – 12); **white** (13 – 14); and **light brown** (23 – 28). The Right colourway is **white** (e.g.1 – 4); **mid grey** (5 – 8); **dark grey** (9 –12); **black** (13–18); and **light grey** (19–20). **Rows 3, 11, 19, 27, 35, 43, 51, 59, 67 and 71-72 are "Inwards" pattern rows - see chart, page 21.**

Vintage Hap Shawl Variation 1 made "Borders Outwards"

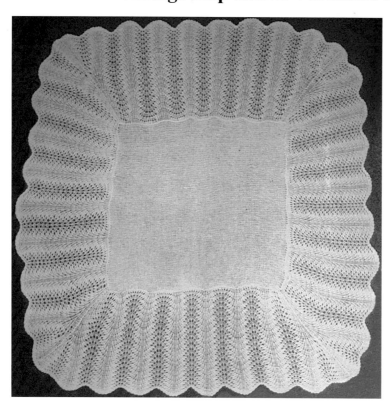

Here is an interesting vintage version of a square un-edged hap, (1940s – 1960s) which is knitted in 400g (14½ oz) of a double-knit butter coloured thicker wool - not Shetland, probably a Yorkshire worsted with 4mm / UK 8 / US 5 - 6 needle.

This shawl has a 8 Hole, 4 Row Old Shell pattern with 4 regularly decreased borders 'close laced' (tightly sewn) together so there are no gaps.

It is a 48 Row Repeat Pattern – so when you get to Row 48, you need to work Rows 1 - 22 again for each border. (72 rows).

For a "flipped" version of this chart to knit outwards, see page 51. This shawl would be beautiful shaded.

Size: 56 inches / 142cm square.

Dressed Tension over garter stitch: 16sts x 32 rows / 4ins / 10cm.

The four Borders each start by casting on very loosely (24 + [7 x 24 = 168] + 24) + (3+4) side sts = **223 sts** (see text below chart) and these are decreased by a 'k2 tog' at both sides of every even row, until there are 151 sts. All border stitches were then cast off loosely. A separately made garter stitch square of 150 stitches x 300 rows was closely sewn to these border tops and then their side flaps stitched together, to make a sturdy shawl. To be extra sure of sturdiness, the outside edge was further crocheted round with "2 single crochet, 3 treble crochet" to give a decorative, protective edge. One border bore a ribbon-woven laundry label or possibly, a country-of-origin label - *France*. Once washed and "de-bitted" by removing the little pill balls, the shawl looked almost as good as new, a testament to working with good pure yarn! In contrast to this one's plain simplicity, the next example is a fancier and finer version.

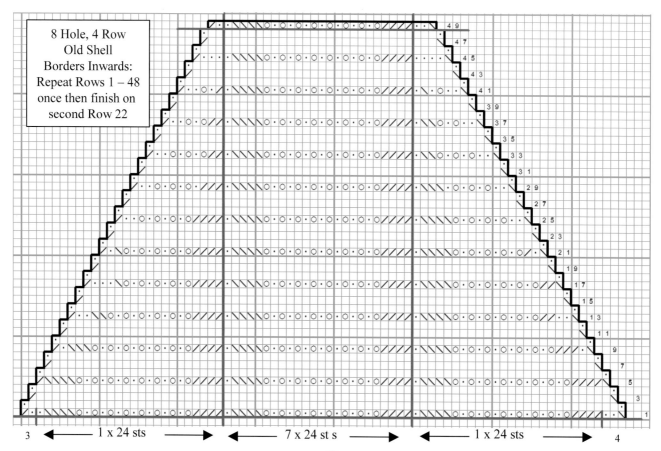

8 Hole, 4 Row Old Shell Borders Inwards: Repeat Rows 1 – 48 once then finish on second Row 22

3   ← 1 x 24 sts →   ← 7 x 24 st s →   ← 1 x 24 sts →   4

Vintage Hap Shawl Variation 2 ~ A 'Half Hap'
made 'Borders Outwards'

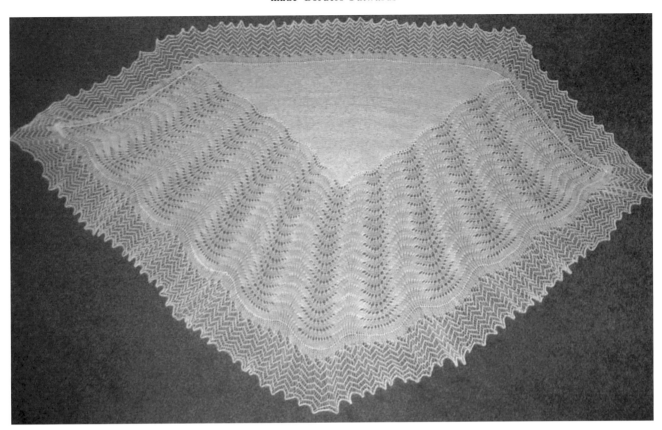

A 'half hap', 'half shawl', 'half square' or "point"* was a frequently made Victorian Shetland shawl form, and the vintage White Shetland Cobweb one above is made with a diagonally knit triangle centre (cast on a stitch, add a new stitch each row, see page 23), usually:

"**wool round needle, knit to end**" until size of triangle is met.

Then here, the two borders are knitted as one "outwards", for the above shawl and an edging knitted round the <u>entire</u> outside. I'm not sure if the Shetland knitters mentioned in the *1872 Truck Report* (see page 54) made their 'half square' haps in this manner; I think it's possible that they'd have made the borders in the traditional "inwards" way as they did for the 'coarser' shawls. This version has a border made in the manner of the Circular Shawl in *Heirloom Knitting, 2002*; and so it has a graduating 4 Row lace-hole pattern throughout. It starts as a '8 Hole' and progresses to a '10 Hole', then finishes as a '12 Hole' lace pattern at the edge, to accommodate the growing expanse and shaping of the virtually semicircular border. The edging pattern used here is a Victorian Frilled Lace Edging, see page 43.

Size: 36 x 72 inches / 90 x 180 cm. UK 12 /2.5mm / US 1 needle; 4oz / 106g Merino Wool, c1/14.5NM = a Shetland Cobweb 1 Ply wool. This would be gorgeous in variegated /random dyed yarn or with shaded borders!

*"The real Shetland is much more fleecy looking than the other kind. ... The price of these shawls ranges from twenty-five and thirty dollars.... The wool for these shawls is not spun, it is washed and picked out in threads; these threads, which are not over a quarter of a yard in length, are tied together and knit by hand. Points, or half shawls of the real Shetland are very elegant." *Godey's Lady's Book, June, 1864. I think the author is describing rooing and hand combing, see page 12.*

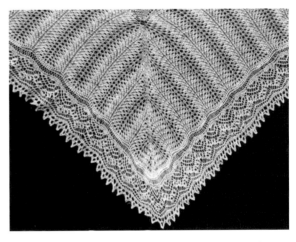

This "Borders Outwards" square shawl (with a diamond centre) is from *Heirloom Knitting, 2002*. It could be made as a half hap using Shetland Cobweb and suitable needles - for needle example, see text left.

Make a triangle centre as described until there's 101 x 2 = 202 sts. Leave these centre stitches on a thread. Tie a bow through the centre with a length of wool so the bow shows on the "front" only - this is handy to make sure both borders are knitted with their fronts matching!

Make each of the two borders separately:

From a centre's side pick up (US: "pick up and knit") 101 sts (4 x 24 sts) + 5 side sts, and follow border pattern chart, page 51, until the borders are as deep as you'd like - e.g. 14 to 18 lace hole columns deep. Knit 4 more plain rows then finish with a decrease row of 'knit 2, k2tog' to get rid of ¼ of the stitches. Sew in ends and up border seam. Knit an edging round the entire shawl and dress.

Some Hap Shawls of Today
– all made "Borders Outwards"

2 ply Grey Shawl – a border corner is shown right, below. This shawl border (see page 30) has a 6 Hole, 6 Row pattern with a Diamond centre and the edging as shown next page.

Tension over dressed garter stitch centre : 18 sts x 16 rows = 4 inches/10cm. For the 54 inch /137cm size:
Jamieson & Smith's Shetland Lace-weight 2 Ply:

      10 x 25g Light Grey (no. L 203)
      1 x 25g Dark Grey (no. L 54)
      2 x 25g Mid Grey   (no. L27)
      1 x 25g White/Cream (no. L1A)

**3.50mm / UK 9 / US 4 Circular Needle :
40 or 60cm (16" or 24") long**

The Cora Shawl – "blues" colour way shown below right. Cora has a traditional shaded border but a centre with a simple flowered lace pattern for interest.

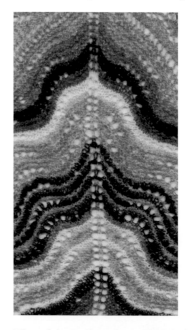

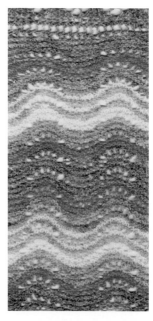

The dainty **Summer Shawl** left, is knitted in Shetland Cobweb 1 ply with a diamond shaped garter stitched centre and has a variation of Old Shell (Crest Of the Wave) short border before the stitches are cast off using a lacy stitch. There's no reason at all why coloured stripes can't be worked in this, and it would be lovely made with a pink or blue edge.

Other Traditional Hap Edgings

Traditional Peaked Edging

Using Waste Wool Cast On cast on 17 edging stitches to the left hand needle: (**Tip!** Use an oddment of yarn and cast on and knit one row before joining in main yarn for edging. Remove the oddment's cast on at end before sewing together.)

Now, begin to work the edging's pattern stitches as shown on the edging chart along the **border sides**, on each return row - towards the border, "knit two together" using the last edging stitch with the next left-over border stitch in turn (**this stitch is shown as shaded symbol on chart. In a straight edging strip, this would be a simple 'knit' stitch**). Gradually, all the border stitches will be cast off as the edging is worked along. When you have finished knitting, graft the two ends of the edging together. If you don't want to attempt grafting, you could cast off the stitches loosely and sew them together instead.

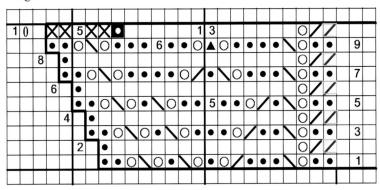

Cast on 17 stitches

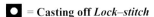 = **Casting off** *Lock–stitch*

When you cast off (US: "bind off"), you have to knit the next stitch along to pass the first cast off stitch over; this anchor stitch I call the "lock -stitch"; because it stops the casting off undoing itself. When you cast off 5 stitches, the lock stitch is the stitch the <u>fifth</u> cast off stitch is passed over - so here, it's the <u>sixth</u> from the beginning of the cast off row.

Two Lace Hole Edgings

This is a much loved traditional hap edging, and can be 3 or 6 'Holed' or more – chart for the usual '6 Holed' version, photographed below. Right Chart: The '3 Hole Edging' for the Koli Shawl, shown on page 10: cast on 19 sts.

The "-" symbol means "purl"; so "knit and purl" into the previous row's double increase (OO). **Tip!** You could simply do one single loose "O" instead on the odd rows, so long as you make the 2 sts on the even rows to keep the stitch count right.

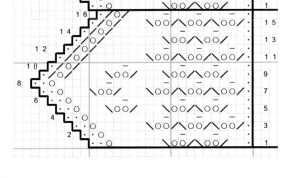

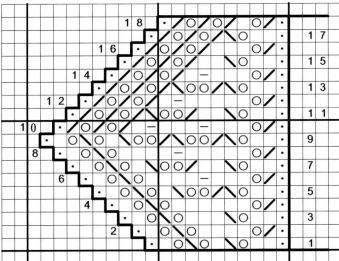

Cast on 10 stitches

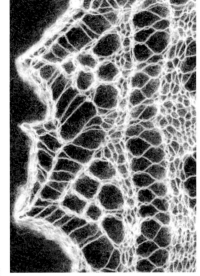

6 Holes Edging

Victorian Frilled Lace Edging

Here are two versions of the same pattern. One for fine haps, below – this was used for the Half Hap, page 41. Right, is one for thicker haps which is a "lace knitting" version, as it has plain rows alternating with pattern rows. The one below is for "knitted lace". Cast on 18 stitches.

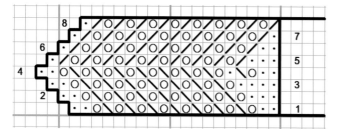

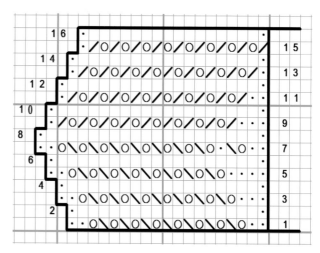

Two More Tips

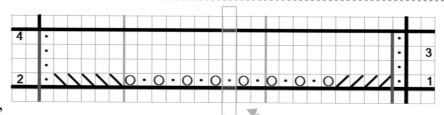

Old Shell "Centre Stitch"

Old Shell has an **easy-to-recognise** *centre stitch* – for a '6 Hole' pattern such as that right, *it's the one after the third 'make 1' or 'hole', in each of the pattern repeats* of that row. See photo and the knitting charts where it's shown. A quick way to identify it is that there are three eyelets ('holes') each side. *For an '8 Hole' pattern such as that charted above, the centre stitch has 4 lace 'holes' each side.*

These will all line up <u>vertically</u> when the pattern is correctly worked; similarly, the six/eight "knit 2 togs" will line up as well.

Get in to the habit of checking that these are in the correct places as you knit; if they're not, it's a good indicator that you've dropped a stitch or something in that section, so spend a moment in putting it right - by counting and re-knitting that block of rows, as necessary, to correct that section of pattern.

The <u>centre stitch</u>

Expert's Tip on Joining Yarn

When **joining in coloured yarn**, knit with the old colour to the exact point you want the colour change to be. Break off the old yarn exactly 6 inches/15cm from this point. Now, undo the stitches you have just made for about 20 stitches, so you have a length of old yarn to manipulate.

Knot in the new colour yarn (Picture 1) exactly six inches/15cm away from the old colour's end - this should now be exactly where the colour change will be in the knitting. Untwist the plies in both colours and break off one ply just after the knot (Picture 2). Bend back the free ply and re-twist it round its same-coloured yarn, then holding the ply ends in place, resume knitting.

I won't pretend this isn't fiddly, but it's worth the practicing, try it out before you use it on the shawl!

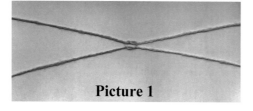

Picture 1

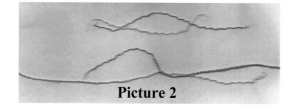

Picture 2

A '6 Hole, 6 Row' Hap Border Chart

see text, page 19

Compare this with Chart on page 18, which is of a 6 Hole, 8 Row pattern.
This one would make a lacier border as it has three more pattern rows.
<u>Star symbols</u> mean 'reserve sts' or do 2 plain rows (82 Rows)
and then a Break Pattern - see page 19, as required.

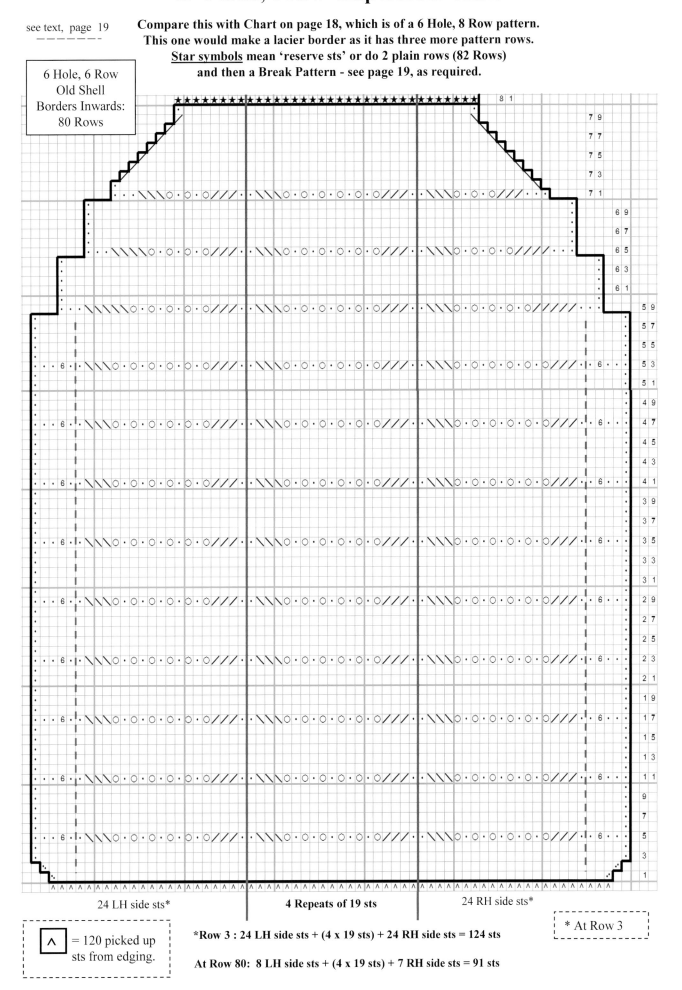

6 Hole, 6 Row
Old Shell
Borders Inwards:
80 Rows

24 LH side sts*   **4 Repeats of 19 sts**   24 RH side sts*

∧ = 120 picked up sts from edging.

*Row 3 : 24 LH side sts + (4 x 19 sts) + 24 RH side sts = 124 sts

At Row 80: 8 LH side sts + (4 x 19 sts) + 7 RH side sts = 91 sts

* At Row 3

Hap Scarves

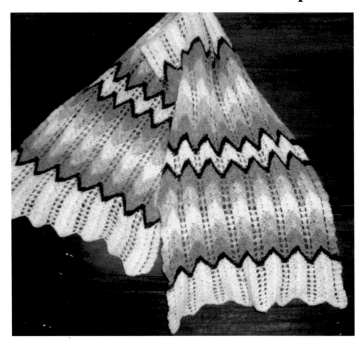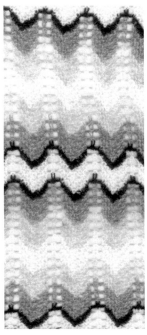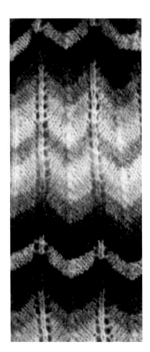

These two 'coarse', coloured scarves were both made in Shetland (c1930-1950) and example some of the simplest items of their traditional lace trade; these were often called hap scarves (Sarah Don). Both show signs of moth attack and felting, and on this ground alone they would have been discarded by most - but fortunately for me, these were rescued by a far-sighted Orkney lady who collected local pieces of knitwear. I'm very interested in their typical colour banding arrangements for these items which are strikingly similar to those used on haps, and these examples could be used as inspirations for hap shawl banding. A third subtly simple beautiful scarf colourway is given on the extreme right above. This could be for a grey based hap: it has regular 4 row bands of (1) light brown (2) mid brown (3) dark brown; (4) Shetland black and (5th and main colour) grey. These colours are then reflected once; and then (6) "white-grey-white" bands form the centre before the sequence is repeated. Both charted scarves were made in coloured Shetland wool – the top shaded one is made in a fine lace weight 2 ply and uses some of the natural colours of Shetland sheep; the bottom smaller scarf is made in chemically dyed 1 ply.

This coloured scarf measured 6 x 30 inches when dressed (15 x 45 cm). The shaded scarf is bigger:12 x 36 inches (30 x 90 cm). Both are made to the charted pattern shown next page, and were knitted as a continuous piece and <u>not</u> in two identical halves grafted together; you can tell this by looking carefully at the top and bottom edges: you should see that in each, the cast on edge has solid points and the cast off edge has lacy points, if either of the scarves had been a grafted piece there'd have been two exactly matching cast on ends. You could make a scarf with two matching halves but simply grafting them together could make for a bumpy join as the delayed increases that form peaks in the pattern would 'fight' each other as they wouldn't happily interlock - you would get round this by designing in a garter stitch neck centre panel which would 'absorb' the pattern's shaping, see diagram right, arrows show direction of knitting.

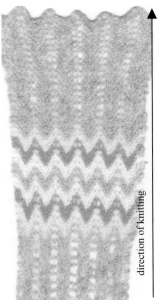

direction of knitting

garter stitch Neck

2 Shetland Razor Shell Scarves

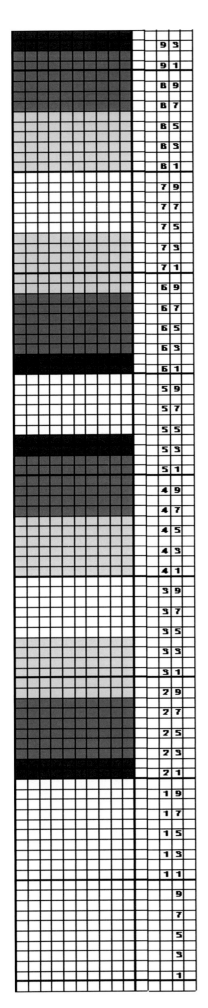

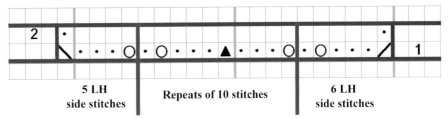

5 LH side stitches   Repeats of 10 stitches   6 LH side stitches

Suggested Needle Size and Tension
Laceweight 2 ply - UK 11 / 3mm / US 2 :   26 sts by 24 rows = 4 ins (10cm)
1 Ply Cobweb   -   UK 11 / 3mm / US 2 :   46 sts by 34 rows = 4 ins (10cm)

Pattern as shown by the 2 row chart above proceeding for each scarf as follows:
Pattern Row 1: K2tog., knit 3, make 1, knit1, * make 1, knit 3, slip 1, k2tog, p.s.s.o., knit 3, make 1, knit 1,**. Repeat to last 5 sts: make 1, knit 3, k2tog.

Shaded Lace weight 2 ply Scarf

4 colours: Cream, Dark Brown, Donkey Brown, Beige and **White**
(or 4 others of your choice)

Cast on 7 repeats of 10 sts + 5 LH and 6 RH side sts = **81 sts**

Follow pattern chart above changing colours as shown by colour chart left:

Work 20 rows in **cream**, then * (74 coloured rows of **dark brown, donkey brown, beige** and **cream, Rows 21-94**) then 14 rows of **cream****.

Repeat from * to **, end with 6 cream rows to match start, loosely cast off.

Coloured Fine 1 ply Scarf

5 colours: Beige, Green, Yellow, Pink and **White** (or 5 others of your choice)

Cast on 6 repeats of 10 sts + 5 LH and 6 RH side sts = **71 sts**

Follow pattern chart above changing colours as shown by colour chart right:

Work 16 rows in **beige**, then * (36 coloured rows of **green, yellow, bright pink** and **white**) then 14 rows of **beige****

Repeat from *to ** twice (to get three coloured bands) then finish with 2 more rows of beige and loosely cast off.

For both scarves:
Sew in all ends and dress.

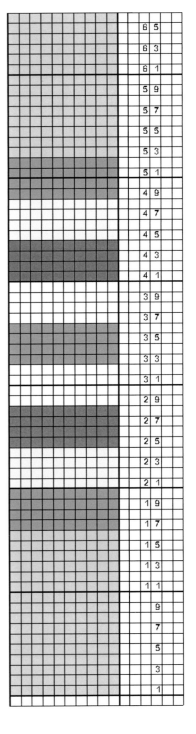

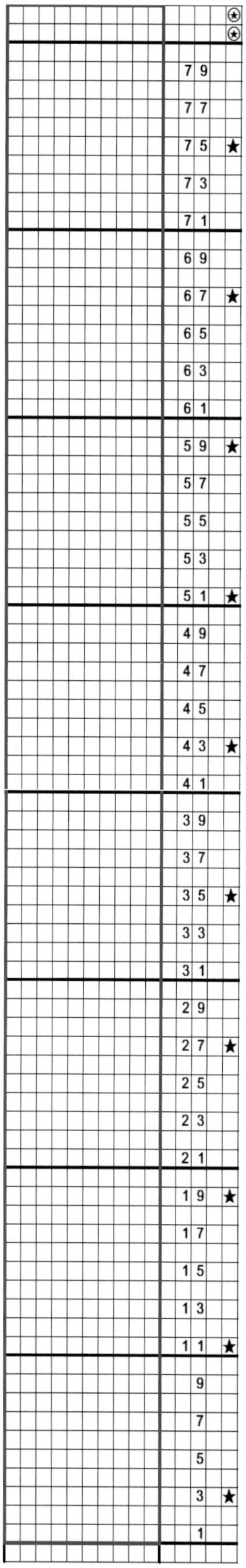

Two Unusual Hap Shawls

DRYING SHETLAND SHAWLS

Here are two unusual haps. Above is a very dramatic and striking colourway for an Old Shell border, the shawl appears to be a dark brown or black one with even gradations of shades from very dark to white before going straight onto the dark brown/black centre in quite an eye-popping manner, without any traditional grading back to dark again. I'd estimate the shadings are in regular 8 row groupings. I've never seen this non-symmetrical bordering done before or since, the photograph dates to around 1930 - 1940. Note the small white hap at the back, that's like the one given in this book.

Below, three very companionable knitters sit together and are obviously chatting happily one breezy day c 1950 I guess, before they were caught in time by the photographer. Although knitting what's termed "Fair Isle" work, two are wearing old haps that are both home washed and dried "undressed", so the lace patterns aren't pointed and open, but gently scallop-edged. The older woman wears a hap with a Tree motif border, note how she's wearing it crossed with the ends tucked in under her skirt band at the side. Again, this is an unusual hap because of its choice of lace border instead of Old Shell; but as a clearly locally made and worn shawl with comparatively plain lace pattern – it's definitely a hap for me!

Shetland Knitters

A Border Colours Template – see page 26. Photocopy off this chart and colour it to suit for your own border design.

Stars = Pattern Rows.
Circle stars = Break Pattern for an 82 row border.

The chart (right-hand column markings):

- ⊛ (circle star)
- ⊛ (circle star)
- 7 9
- 7 7
- 7 5 ★
- 7 3
- 7 1
- 6 9
- 6 7 ★
- 6 5
- 6 3
- 6 1
- 5 9 ★
- 5 7
- 5 5
- 5 3
- 5 1 ★
- 4 9
- 4 7
- 4 5
- 4 3 ★
- 4 1
- 3 9
- 3 7
- 3 5 ★
- 3 3
- 3 1
- 2 9
- 2 7 ★
- 2 5
- 2 3
- 2 1
- 1 9 ★
- 1 7
- 1 5
- 1 3
- 1 1 ★
- 9
- 7
- 5
- 3 ★
- 1

Knitting Advice

How To Graft the Edging's Start and Finish Together

Grafting (Weaving – U.S.) is the technical name for producing by sewing, a join identical to a row of knitting. It is also known in one form as Kitchener Stitch. Make sure you have the same number of stitches on both sides of knitting to be joined. Keep both sets of stitches on the knitting needles – it's a useful tip to transfer both sets of stitches to a larger sized pair of needles or on a contrasting thread to stop them slipping off so readily. You could also give a coat of spray starch to the stitches to help stop them unravelling. Thread a blunt tapestry needle with sufficient wool – about three times the length to be grafted.

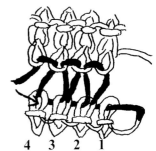

top needle stitches

4 3 2 1
bottom needle stitches

Make sure your rows of knitting to be grafted resemble exactly the above drawing – knit (or purl) an extra row if necessary. N.B. The stitches are shown 'off the pins' for clarity. Keep them on the pin/needle until you have been through each stitch at least once. (Note, that apart from the first and last stitch, you go into every stitch loop *twice* before slipping it off the needle/contrast thread).

I give the **Garter Stitch Method for Grafting** here, refer to above diagram:

*On the bottom needle, sew *down* through the first stitch and *up* through the second stitch. Next, on the top needle, sew *up* through the first stitch and *down* through the second stitch. Withdraw the first stitches from both needles. Repeat from * (the second stitches on both needles have now become 'first stitches'). Regularly pull the sewing yarn through the stitches to lie in place. Grafting, I think, is one of the hardest processes of knitting, but it is well worth practising first and consulting the knitting reference books to achieve the desired best effects.

How to Dress the Shawl

'Dressing'(Blocking U.S.) is the name that is given to the final processing of a Shetland lace item. Using a wool detergent, wash and rinse the shawl in a basin in tepid water. DO NOT RUB, WRING OR CHANGE THE WATER TEMPERATURE AS THIS MAY CAUSE FELTING OR SHRINKAGE!

Using a clean, colourfast towel to wrap the shawl in, blot up the excess water till it is damp but not dripping wet. Pull shawl gently to shape on a flat surface and pay special attention to pulling out gently each point of the edging before pinning tautly. (Obviously, keep animals and children away and warn any others that you have used pins, I use quilters pins with large coloured glass heads for this task, as they are easier both to fix and retrieve later).

Leave till shawl is thoroughly dry away from heat or sunlight, this will take several hours – I dry my shawls on the double bed – a cool electric fan may be used to speed up the drying. As a final word, save the remaining wool and pattern and keep with the shawl so they are to hand if you need to make a repair at any time. Enjoy!

Alternatively use Dressing Wires, which are fine and long stainless steel rods to thread the points on and stretch the knitting to shape, see them in use, page 26.

This is a 2 Ply Grey Shawl being dressed with pins to a large bed. Dressing was the last process before a shawl went for sale. But for the 1900s spinner here, dressing seems to have been an extra cost or trouble to be avoided if possible. Like the haps of almost all Shetland women shown in this book, her tattered hap is undressed; and she is clearly careworn and weather-beaten, testimony to the hard working life she and other spinners and knitters led. The contrast between the ethereal beauty of Shetland lace (of which I believe the hap can be seen as the prototype in construction) and the circumstances of their makers was often a point for comment by late 19th century visitors to the islands, and one we can still appreciate today. Extracts from the Truck Report of 1872 follow, and are worth reading to see just how remarkable a tradition Shetland knitting was and is.

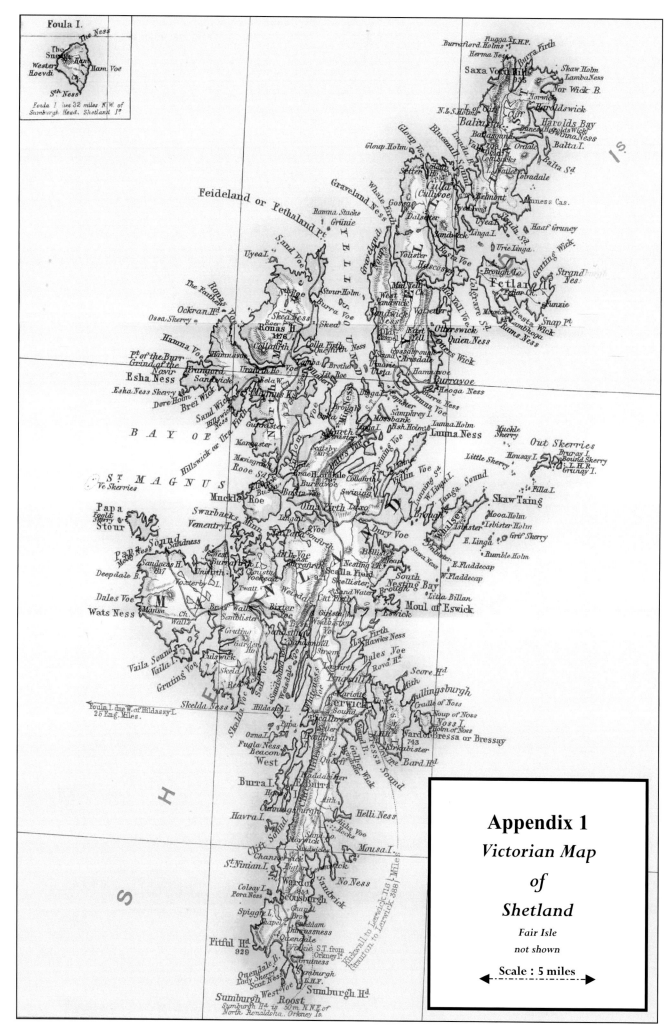

Appendix 1

Victorian Map

of

Shetland

Fair Isle
not shown

Scale : 5 miles

Appendix 2
The Word 'Hap' in Scotland

"I pray you will send me two ells of worsted for doublets, to happe me this cold winter." John (?) Paston to his cousin Margaret Paston; an extract requesting two lengths of tightly spun woollen cloth for him to have made into jackets. An ell in England was 45 inches. *The Paston Letters, 1461 –1465*, were written at the time of The English "Wars of the Roses" 1455-1487. Now the word has dropped from everyday use in English.

Below though, are two traditional songs showing the use of 'hap' in dialect as a verb and a noun and it's a word still in common use in Scotland today. For sales to 'Southerners' in the 19th century, the dialect word was considered too archaic and was often replaced by 'wrap', 'coarse' or 'stout', so haps were typically called 'Winter', 'Wrap' or 'Stout Shawls'.

COME UNDER MY PLAIDY
'Come under my plaidy, the night's ga'en to fa';
Come in frae the cauld blaft, the drift and the fnaw;
Come under my plaidy, and lye down befide me;
There's room in't dear lafsie, believe me for twa
Come under my plaidy, and lye down befide me
I'll <u>hap</u> ye frae ev'ry cauld blaft that will blaw.
O come under my plaidy, and lye down befide me
there's room in't dear lafsie be-lieve me for twa.'

(Hector MacNeill 1746 –1818)

HAP ME WI' THY PETTICOAT
'O Bell, thy looks have kill'd my heart,
I pafs the day in pain
When night returns, I feel the fmart.
And wifh for thee in vain.
I'm ftarving cold whilft thou art warm,
Have pity and incline,
And grant me for a <u>hap</u>
That Charming pet-ti-coat of thine.'

(Possibly a 1720s song)

From traditional songs collected by James Johnson and Robert Burns and published as
Scots Musical Museum
Blackwood & Sons, 1853

ƒ = old letter 's'   'Plaidy' = plaid blanket/clothing cloth

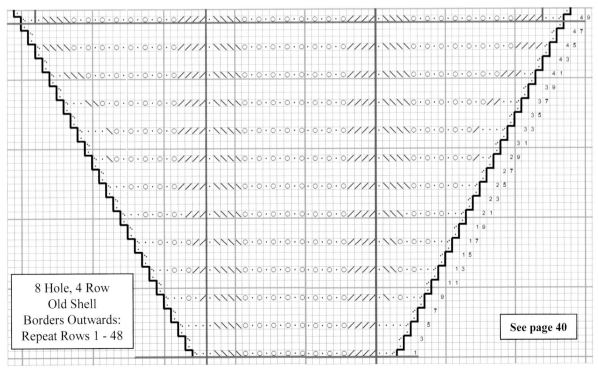

8 Hole, 4 Row
Old Shell
Borders Outwards:
Repeat Rows 1 - 48

See page 40

Appendix 3

Evidence Regarding Haps from the 1872 Truck Inquiry

I include these passages as I found it fascinating to hear the actual knitters and traders speak in their own words: sometimes guarded, or rarely, defiant – but almost invariably one feels, respectful of the truth. The actual report extends to over 400 pages of very close print, and lots of evidence is taken regarding housing, kelp-burning, fishing, crofting, whaling, sealing, rents, the price of goods and of course, the hosiery (knitting) trade; and everything else investigating Sheriff Guthrie thought relevant. A lot of witnesses were called, many were clearly afraid to answer for fear of offending the merchants / landlords to whom they were deeply indebted. Still, through the evidence, one can get a clearer picture of the lives of the knitters themselves, and it's worth reading the report to appreciate the real struggle of the Shetlanders day-to-day life then. Below, I also reproduce selected extracts regarding the makers and sellers of 'coarse shawls', a local description of haps.

It will help readers to know that the hap knitters generally had an extremely hard time of it in Lerwick, they were working often with the merchant's yarn and only getting credit against their work which they had to take in 'soft goods' (drapery) or in pricier stock such as soap or tea, where the merchants would make the most profit. For country knitters it seems slightly better, as they usually had their own supply of yarn and local produce; so often, they'd take the merchants' bartered tea etc, and then make exchanges with country farmers for cash at a discount, or for other food such as meat.

On the counter side, many merchants acted charitably and although they roundly claim to despise the old barter system they almost all ran, as it was 'profitless' and troublesome to them; they continued to do so on the quiet, certainly up to the 1940s. It did provide a means of real employment for many women who would otherwise have been destitute. The finer lace knitting rightly attracted the best prices but it was very time consuming and the returns still poor; so, many knitters seemed almost forced to produce small 'coarser' items regularly to survive and consequently, the quality of some of these could be below that readily saleable, which further cut the returns they had for their work and also diminished demand. A difficult situation, as the indefatigable and conscientious Sheriff Guthrie as Commissioner will conclude.

Text Note: *Weights, and lengths are in Imperial quantities:* **WEIGHT** *: pounds and ounces;* **LENGTH** *: feet and yards. Sterling* **MONEY** *: penny (d.), shilling (s.) and pound (£.). It was '12 pennies to 1 shilling' and '20 shillings to 1 pound': Approximates here are from the Retail Prices Index (RPI), ref: Laurence H. Officer "Comparing the Purchasing Power of Money in Great Britain from 1264 – 2005", Economic History Series, 2005.*

E.g.: The 1870's **£1 = £64** *in 2005's currency, and* **1d.** *(a 'penny') then = 2005's* **'27p.'** *½ d. =* **'13p.'** *(2005)* **6d.** *('sixpence' or ½ shilling) = 2005's* **'£1.59p.'** *and* **1s** *= 2005's* **'£3.19p.'**

So, a knitter bartering a 72 inch 'big shawl' hap for the1870's 10s, would receive the equivalent of £32 (2005 RPI). A pittance.

The Sheriff's numbered questions are typed here in **Bold** – Answers follow. *(SM: My comments are in blue italics for this Appendix and so 'SM' = Sharon Miller).* --

PREAMBLE : "THE Report on the Truck System, presented to Parliament in 1871, stated that the Commissioners, Messrs. Bowen and Sellar, had received information from four witnesses with regard to Shetland,'tending to show that the existence of Truck in an oppressive form is general in the staple trades of the islands'. The Commissioners in their Report call attention to this evidence, and add: 'Time would not allow of a local inquiry at Shetland, nor can an inquiry be adequately conducted into the Truck which is alleged to prevail there otherwise than upon the spot. No opinion accordingly is offered either as to the extent of, or the remedy for, the alleged evils; but the necessity of some investigation by Her Majesty's Government into the condition of these islands seems made out.'

Having been appointed, by a warrant under your hand, dated Dec. 23, 1871, one of the Commissioners under the Truck Commission Act, 1870, in room of Mr. Bowen, I was directed to proceed to Shetland and institute an inquiry there under that Act........(William Guthrie)

Lerwick, January 1, 1872, BARBARA JOHNSTON, examined.

364. You have come from the parish of Sandwick?-Yes. **365. How far is that from Lerwick?**- About thirteen miles. *(SM: West Yell.)* **366. Who do you live with there?**- I live with my mother, Mrs. Johnston. My father is dead. **367. How many of a family are there of you?**- I have two brothers and a sister in the south and there is a sister at home besides myself.

368. You do some work in knitting?-Yes. **369. For whom do you work?**- For Mr. Robert Linklater. **370. Do you always work for him?**- Yes. I work for nobody else. **371. Have you a pass-book?**- No. *(SM: This seems to be a description of a small credit book recording transactions between merchant and knitter, this merchant is in Lerwick).* **372. How long have you worked for Mr. Linklater?**- For some years. I cannot say the number exactly.

373. Do you get wool from him, or do you supply it yourself?- I get the worsted from him, and I am paid by him for my work. **374. What kind of wages do you get?**- I get 10s. for making a big shawl. **375. That is not the finest quality of knitting?**- No; it is about the coarsest. **376. Is it always shawls that you work at?**- No; sometimes I make veils. *(SM: This would be veils for hats, therefore quite small with tiny lace patterns, see 'More Heirloom Knitting', now in production. 'Coarsest' = a thicker wool yarn used for haps, but still not thicker than c 106 yds per oz / 84m per 25g. A 'big shawl' would be over 72 inches / 180cm square).*

377. When you take your work back to Mr. Linklater, are you paid for it in money or in goods?- In goods. **378. Do you sometimes ask for money?-** Yes. **379. What has he said to you when you asked for money?-** He says he never gives it, and that he won't give it to me. I got 2s. from him today; but that is all I ever got, except, I think, one sixpence before. I also got the offer of a pass-book to-day. I had never been offered one before. **380. Was it after you had seen me this forenoon that you got the 2s. and the offer of the pass-book?-** Yes. *(SM: Sheriff Guthrie obviously thinks he sees a connection between the Inquiry and the offer of money and pass-book!)*

381. When you get your worsted, is there a bargain made between the merchant and you about the payment you are to receive for the work?- No. I have just an idea what I think the thing will come to; and then, when I come back with it, he gives me what he likes. **382. You don't make any bargain beforehand?-** No. **383. But you might do so if liked?-** He won't do it. I have asked him, but he said he would see the thing when I came back with it.

384. I suppose, he wants to see the quality of the work before he pays for it?-Yes. **385. Did you take the pass-book that was offered you today?-** No. **386. Why?-** I had no particular reason for not taking it. **387. Did you not want it?-** I thought I would not mind it to-day, as I had never had one before. **388. Do you remember the last time before to-day when you went to Mr. Linklater with some of your work?-** Yes. **389. How much was due to you at that time?-** I think he was due me about £1. **390. That would be for more than one shawl?-** Yes; it was for some veils about four months ago. I have made two shawls for him since, and some veils. **391. But the last time you went with your work, how much was due you?-** I think there would be about £1. **392. Did you ask for money then?-** Yes. **393. Who did you ask it from?-** Mr. Linklater.

394. Was it from Mr. Linklater himself, or one of his people?- It was either from Mr. Linklater or from Mr. Anderson; I don't remember which. **395. What was said to you?-** He just said that he would not give it, as he never gave any. **396. What goods did you get?-** Some stuff for a dress, and some tea and cotton. **397. Had you made up your mind before you went there as to what you wanted to buy?-** Yes. **398. And you got what you wanted?-** I had to take what he had. I had no other chance. **399. Did you want these goods at that time?-** If I had got the money, I would not have bought them at that time. **400. What would you have done with the money?-** I would have bought grocery things - things that he did not have……..

419. How much money did you ask for to-day?- I asked for 2s., and I got it. **420. Did you not want more?-** I did not ask more and I don't think I would have got more if I had asked it. That was the reason why I did not ask it; because Mr. Linklater does not make it his practice give money. **421. Then when you go in any day to the merchant, you just say, 'Here is your shawl,' and you ask how much you are to get for it?-** Yes. **422. What is his answer?-** He just mentions whatever he likes to give. **423. But he gives you a fair value for the work, does he?-** Yes; sometimes. **424. Do you think he puts too low a value on your work?-** Yes; I often think that. **425. Do you think there is anything very unreasonable in the value he puts upon it?-** Yes; sometimes I do.

426. How long does it take you to make a 10s. shawl - I would make one of them in a month if I was not doing much else. ………**442. Were you thinking of not dealing with Mr. Linklater any more?-** No; I have got another shawl from him to make. **443. Did you get the worsted for it to-day?-** Yes.

444. Does Mr. Linklater take a note of the quantity of worsted he gives out to you?- Yes; he weighs it. **445. He knows how much it will take to make a shawl, and he weighs the shawl when it is brought back?-**Yes. **446. Have you ever bought worsted for your own knitting?-** No; I could not get it bought, because I was not in the way of earning money. **447. Have you tried to buy it?-** I could not try without the money. He would not give worsted for nothing. **448. And you had no money to pay for it?-** No; I could not have it.

449. But when you were taking back your work to him, have you never asked to take part of the value of it in worsted?- I have; and I have been refused. **450. When did you do that?-** It is long ago now; but I have done it....*(SM: "he said")*... that it was a money article and he could not give it without the money. ………I only remember asking it once. I never did it again, when I got a denial the first time. ………I would like to speak on my sister's behalf as well as my own. She is not here, but she wants to say the same thing that I have done. **455. She wants to make the same complaint?-** Yes. She is not well, and is unable to come in.

ARTHUR LAURENSON, examined.

2120. You are a partner of the firm of Laurenson & Co., Shetland warehousemen and clothiers in Lerwick?- I am. ……..**2126. In the Shetland hosiery business you get the goods from the women knitters, who I believe are of two classes: those who knit for you, and those who sell to you?-** Yes. There are those who bring the article and just exchange it over the counter. The greater part of our business now consists in the exchanging of goods, rather than in the employing of women to knit for us. Some years ago we were more in that way than we are now. Our principal business now just consists in buying their own productions, or rather, I should say, in the exchanging of them.

2127. By using the word exchanging, what is it that you mean to imply?- I mean to make a difference between that and buying for actual cash. If I were using the word, buying, it might convey the idea that we pay cash down. When I say exchanging, I mean that they bring us the article, and we give them other articles in exchange for it. **2128. By that you mean to imply that the transaction is understood as a barter?-** Precisely. **2129. What is the character of the stock that you keep?-** Drapery articles altogether, and general soft goods. The only grocery goods we keep are tea and soap…

2330. Can you not give what would be about the average?- I will give an instance. About a fortnight ago I bought a shawl from a girl for 35s., made of common Yorkshire wool. *(SM: See Mr Walker's evidence later, page 58, regarding yarn.)* It was her own material, and she just came in with it, and sold it over the counter. The material of that shawl, for which I gave her 35s., had not cost her 4s. It was a half-square shawl. (*SM: A term for 'half hap'.*) It is still lying in the shop, and I can produce it if it is desired. The whole value of that article depended on the workmanship contained in it.

2331. Is it a black or white shawl?- White. It is not even fine Shetland worsted, which is the most valuable sort of thing.
2332. Is fine Shetland worsted more valuable than the other worsted at 32s?- Yes, we can always get a better price; and indeed the article is much more valuable when made of fine white Shetland wool than of fine white English wool, because there is a hardness and coarseness in the English wool that is not in the Shetland.

2333. But you don't pay so much as 32s. per pound for Shetland wool in any case?- No, I doubt think we pay so much as that for it, but the Shetland wool is more rare. The supply of it is limited. You can get any quantity of mohair or alpaca, but you cannot get any quantity of fine Shetland wool. **2334. Do you purchase that quality of fine Shetland wool to any extent?-** I buy some of it. I have paid as high as 6d. a cut of nominally 100 threads for it; but that was a rare article. 4d. per cut is the usual thing. *(SM: 'cut' – see page 56.)*

Lerwick, January 4, 1872, WILLIAM JOHNSTONE, examined. *(SM: Another Lerwick merchant.)* **2847. I see here 'One brown half hap shawl, 3s. 9d.** *(SM: 'half hap' see page 41)* **: ' would there be a profit upon that?-** There would not be much; perhaps there would be 8d. on it. **2848. 'One large hap, 18s.: ' would you have a profit on that?-** Yes; I might have about 2s. that article was made specially to order. **2849. Was it made with, your own wool?-** Yes.

2850. 'One white hap, 9s. 6d.?'- There might be about 1s. on that hap. **2851. Was it bought over the counter for goods?** - I think that one was made upon an order; but it was paid for by me in goods. **2852. There is another one at 9s. 6d.?-** That is one of the same size and of the same colour. **2853. Suppose that 9s. 6d. hap had not been made to order, but had been bought over the counter and had been settled for with goods, what profit do you suppose would have been upon it apart from the goods?-** I cannot say.

2854. Was 9s. 6d. the price which you paid to the party selling, or was it somewhat less?- It was 8s. 6d., and I would have a profit of a shilling on it. **2855. That was when it was knitted for you?-** Yes.

2856. But I am speaking of articles which were bought by you: what profit would you have upon such an article then?- I could not tell unless I knew the kind of goods they were to take for it. **2857. But apart from the goods altogether, what would you give for a shawl that you would sell for 9s. 6d., if it was offered to you for sale?-** Perhaps I might give 9s. 6d. worth or goods. **2858. Would that be the usual way of dealing?-** Sometimes it is. It depends very much upon the quality of the article. Sometimes we pay a dear price for them, and at other times we get them pretty cheap.

Lerwick, January 6, 1872, ISABELLA SINCLAIR, examined.

3245. You are the daughter of Mr. Sinclair (*SM: A Lerwick Merchant*)**, who has just been examined, and one of the assistants in the shop?-** Yes. **3246. Are you sometimes concerned in the purchase of hosiery goods?-** No; I never purchase hosiery. **3247. You only sell in the shop?-** Yes. ....3292. ..... I see twelve hap-shawls at 11s. 6d.: what would these be bought for across the counter?-** It is very likely that 11s. 6d. would be paid for them in goods. **3293. In this account I see one hap-shawl entered at 14s., and then at 13s.: what does that mean?-** It means that 14s., was paid for it, and it was sold for 13s. Perhaps it may have been slightly ill-coloured.

3294. In the wholesale trade list which has been given in, I see white, brown, and grey shawls, natural colours, charged 8s. 6d. to 18s.: do you know, from what you see in the shop, the prices at which these are generally bought over the counter?- They are just bought at the same prices at which they are invoiced, and which are put down there. **3295. When a shawl is brought to the shop and paid for in goods, is it ticketed for the south market?-** Yes; the fine shawls are ticketed.....

3296. Wrap or winter shawls, 8s. 6d.: would these be ticketed?- No. *(SM: From her later answer, these seem to be haps; I have a 1860/70 "List of Prices" offering "WARM WRAP SHAWLS 20s, in* Shaded Colours, *25s." -my underscoring, must most likely, refer to haps but refrains from using the word as it was not a common one. The list states these were also available as: "Small Size, 7s to 15s." This important price list is from Currie & Co, a truck-free company founded with Royal patronage that only paid cash. Its Shetland founder, a young widow Margaret Curry (nee Colvin), famously intervened on behalf of knitters to get fairer cash prices, and it's even claimed her publicising the plight of Shetland knitters led to this very Truck Inquiry. Initially, she organised private drawing room sales, and later, it seems her company was run by her sisters as 'Schoor & Co.'; and 'Schoor, Muir &Co.'. The company appears to have had the choice of local knitting, and operated for at least 25 years. Later Schoor & Co. felt they* were *able to use the word 'hap' in advertising when offering "WARM INFANT HAPS,* IN WHITE AND GREY. *LARGE WARM HAPS." By the 1890s, 'Wrap Shawls' may also be a description of large thicker garter knit squares with a fancy lace edging and no border – there are illustrations and directions of such 'winter' and 'wrap' shawls in later issues of 1890 + knitting magazines.)*

3297. Why?- Because my father knows the prices so well; they are sold by measure. **3298. The prices at which they are charged do not depend so much on fancy?-** No. **3299. Then the prices of these shawls are fixed afterwards?-** Yes.

3300. How do you know that the prices which are charged for these shawls are the same as have been paid for them over the counter?- Because I have seen haps sold at the counter for 8s. 6d.; and afterwards when they were ready for the market, they were charged at the same, or nearly the same, price. **3301. Don't you sometimes see them charged at a higher price?-** I cannot say exactly, because I do not always notice what the prices are; but I know that I have sometimes seen the same prices charged. I have noticed that particularly in haps. **3302. There are grey and brown long shawls, 20s. to 24s. are these also haps?-** Yes. *(SM: I believe 'long shawls' are here called 'haps', because they were in 'hap' wool and colouring, perhaps like the scarves shown on page 46. A 'long shawl' was also likely then to be called a 'plaid' or 'Double square' shawl. These could be 60" - 70" / 152 cm - 178 cm wide by 120" - 140" / 300 cm - 350 cm long. By the 1850s, it was common for men to wear woven plaids:"We have seen accounts of the gentleman's plaid shawl having become a common article of dress in many places in England, and it is now not seen unfrequently in France. It is beginning to be worn by American gentlemen, and is not now a subject of wonder in our streets." Scientific American, November 13, 1852. Even President Lincoln favoured a long cloth shawl. See also my comment on page 57.)*

3303. Are they generally bought at from 20s. to 24s.?- Yes. **3304. And sold at the same prices?-** Yes, I have noticed that. **3305. You have nothing to do with the pricing of them yourself?-** Nothing at all. I merely see the tickets, and recognise the article. Perhaps there was something particular about it which led me to recognise it. **3306. How often has that happened?-** I could not say. **3307. Has it happened a dozen times?-** It has surely happened more than a dozen times. That is a very small number.

Lerwick, January 6, 1872, JOHN JAMES BRUCE, examined.

3308. Are you a shopman to Mr. Sinclair?-Yes. **3309. You are not the bookkeeper?-**No. ....**3311. Do you also know the prices at which these same goods are invoiced to the southern market?-** Yes. **3312. Is the price at which they are bought and the price at which they are sold the same, or different, on the ordinary run of goods?-**They are charged to the wholesale or the retail dealer in the south at the same price as we pay for them in goods at the counter. **3313. Is that the invariable practice?-**Yes.

3314. The goods, I understand, are not all ticketed when bought?- Fine shawls are generally ticketed, but haps and other goods are judged of afterwards, when being looked out in order to be sent to the market in the south. **3315. In the case of fine shawls, is it within your own knowledge that the ticket put upon them at the time of the purchase bears generally the same price as has been paid for them in goods?-** Yes. Mr Sinclair puts up these goods himself for the market, and the ticket is put on them at the time of the purchase, in order to bring to his remembrance, when he is putting them up for the market, the price he paid for them at the counter.

3316. In all these cases there is only one valuation of the shawl, and it is made to the person who brings it to you for sale?- Yes. **3317. The ticket is put on them, and the invoice price is the same as the price on the ticket?-** Yes, the same. **3318. Do you make no allowance, in that case, for the loss upon the dressing or the dyeing of the shawl?-** When a girl comes with an article that is ill-coloured, she may ask a certain price for it; but we state that we cannot give her that price, owing to it being ill-coloured, and that it requires to be dyed. In that case we deduct the price of the dyeing from the price which is paid to her. **3319. Is that deduction made before the price is put on the ticket?-** We don't ticket it then. It has to be sent south to the dyer, and to come back and to be dressed here. **3320. In that case you must make an estimate, because you cannot identify the shawl afterwards?-** No; we just leave it to our own judgment afterwards. **3321. Then it appears that you don't invoice the goods at exactly the same price that is paid in every case?-** We don't invoice them at the same price if we are selling them to private individuals; but when we sell them to a retail dealer, we invoice them at the same price.

3322. But you have said that very often you require to send them to the dyer, in which case they are not ticketed at the time you purchase them?- No; but the retail dealer must pay for the dyeing. **3323. But the goods are not always ticketed at the time they are bought?-** No; not always. I did not say they were. **3324. Are they ticketed, as a rule, when they are bought?-** The finest of the lace goods or shawls are ticketed. **3325. And veils?-** No, not veils; but the fine lace shawls are generally ticketed.

3326. How is the invoice price of the veils fixed, if they are not ticketed when they are bought?- We can easily judge of the quality of a veil by looking at it, and we can tell what we paid for it. Of course, in fixing the price, we always refer to what we paid for it, and we know that at a glance by the quality of the work and the worsted.... **3330. Are many of the shawls dyed?-** A good many. Some are dyed on account of being ill-coloured. Perhaps we don't discover, at the time when they are taken in over the counter, that they are ill-coloured; we only find that out afterwards, and then we have to dye them. Sometimes we dye shawls, not on account of them being ill-coloured, but because we require them of a particular colour. **3331. Is that done with fine shawls?-** Both with fine and coarse. **3332. But not with haps?-** Sometimes with haps too. We dye haps scarlet and black. **3333. Therefore there is a considerable quantity of the shawl goods which it is not possible to ticket at the time when they are bought, because they have afterwards to be dyed** - Yes, a considerable quantity. **3334. And, in that case, the price is fixed afterwards, according to your own notions of the quality?-** Yes. **3335. Who fixes the invoice price of shawls when they are sent out finally to the market?-** Mr. Sinclair himself. He takes that department. .....**3342. Are you in a position to state whether or not that valuation which is made when they are sent out exceeds the valuation which is put upon them when they are purchased for the market?-** I have reason to believe from Mr. Sinclair's long experience in the trade, that he will know to a fraction what he paid for the shawls; and I can swear that they are not charged by him at a higher price than the price which was paid for them in goods at the counter. Of course deductions are made afterwards by the wholesale dealer, if he thinks the article is inferior.

Lerwick, January 6, 1872, Mrs. ANN EUNSON, examined. *(SM: Sheriff Guthrie seems to suspect she may be a witness sent in by the merchant, certainly she seems to have had favourite treatment compared to some others.)*

3415. You live in Lerwick?-Yes. **3416. You have come forward voluntarily to make a statement?**- Yes. **3417. Nobody has sent you here?**- No. **3418. Have you knitted for a long time to Mr. Linklater?**-Yes, for a long time; I don't remember how long. **3419. What have you made?**- Little hap-shawls. **3420. How have you been paid for them?**- I have been well paid for them, according to what I sought. **3421. Did you get money or goods?**- When I sought money I got it; but when I required anything which he had, I thought it was my duty to take it from him, and not from another. He always gave me a little money when I asked it. **3422. How much would you get at a time?**- I might not ask above 6d. at a time, but I would get it. **3423. How much would you make in a week by knitting?**- It was just as I had time to sit at it.

3424. Did you do a good deal at it?- Not a great deal I made a good many haps for myself when I could. I am a widow. I had seven children, who are all dead, and I have supported myself entirely by my work. **3425. Have you supported yourself entirely by knitting?**- Yes. I had no other work, except that of going for peats, or anything else I had to do. **3426. Were these your own peats?**- Yes. **3427. Therefore you had no other means except by knitting?**- No; except that for some time back I have had 1s. a week from the parochial board. *(SM: 'Poor Relief,' raised by local taxes and paid only to those resident in the parish and normally considered absolutely incapable of work.)*

3428. Before you got that, did you support yourself entirely by knitting?- Yes; only at times I have got some things from friends. **3429. Did you get your meal and provisions from the proceeds of your knitting?**- Yes. **3430. How did you manage that, when you were paid mostly in goods?**- Often, when I had a little time, I made small shawls for myself; and when travelling merchants came to town, they would take my shawls and sell them for me for a little money. **3431. Did you do that because it was not the custom to give money for such things at the merchants' shops?**- It was not the usual thing always to give money at the merchants shops. If they had given it, I might not have given my shawls to these travelling merchants. **3432. If you had got money from the merchants shops, you would have been as ready to sell your shawls to them as to these strangers?**- Yes; but I sold some haps to Mr. Linklater, and got much the same from him as I got from them. **3433. Only you got it in goods?**- Yes; but if had sought a little money, I would have got it. **3434. What was the price of the hap-shawls which you made?**- I have got as high as 3s. and 4s. for them. I don't make the fine knitting. **3435. Do you ever make hose or stockings?**-Yes. **3436. What do you get for them?**- I don't make many stockings; I think I am better paid by making these little haps. *(SM: From her reference to them being 'little' and the price given, these seem to be in the region of 36 inches – 48 inches/ 90 –120cm, for which she would get just over £9.50 to less than £13 in 2005's value.)*

3437. Do you take any lodgers?- I don't take any now. I am in the Widows' Asylum; but before I went there, I took one or two. **3438. Did these lodgers help you in your living?**- Yes, a little. **3439. Then you would get money in that way with which to purchase provisions?**- Yes; but I could not get so much knitting made when I had lodgers. **3440. But the money you got from them would help you to buy meal and bread, and what you wanted to live upon?**- No; I did not have above 6d. a week from my lodgers, and sometimes it was 1s.; but I got through with it, and now it is come to a conclusion. **3441. How old are you?**- I think I am about seventy-two. **3442. You are still knitting a little?**-Yes; my fingers are as clever as can be yet. **3448. You don't get money for your knitting now?**- I get money from Mr. Linklater when I ask it. **3444. How often do you ask it?**- I don't like to trouble him too much, but I know that he would give me what I sought; and many a time I have got it. He often supplied me when I required it, and when I had nothing in his hands to get.

Mid Yell, January 17, 1872, LAURENCE WILLIAMSON, examined.

8993. You are a merchant in this neighbourhood?- Yes; at Linkshouse, Mid Yell. **8994. Have you been long in business there?**- Nearly eight years.......... **9052. Do you buy hosiery?**- A little sometimes. **9053. Do you pay for it in the way that is usual in the country, by goods across the counter?**- Yes, mostly. **9054. Do you give out wool to knit?**- I sometimes give out worsted, and I pay for the knitting of it in the same way. **9055. Have you a knitters' book, or are the knitters' accounts kept in the ledger?**- I keep a book for women's accounts. **9056. Is that book used entirely for sales of hosiery?**- No. We don't do a great deal in hosiery. We buy a few haps and small shawls, but the principal thing we buy is worsted. I buy a good deal in the course year from the spinners, and I sell it chiefly in Lerwick to the merchants there. I sell most of it to Mr. Robert Linklater. I invoice it to the merchants, and I take a note of the quantities when I send them away. **9057. When did you send away the last?**- I suppose it would be about a couple of months ago. **9058. At what price did you send it out?**- We get 3d. per cut for very fine, and 2 ½ d. and 2d. for the coarsest. **9059. You sell to the merchants as a sort of wholesale dealer?**- Yes. **9060. The price per pound of that worsted varies according to the quality?**- Yes. **9061. It does not correspond with the price per cut in any way?**- No. Of course the finer the worsted the finer the thread is. 9062. You do not calculate the price of that worsted, by the pound at all?- No. We just judge of the fineness or the thickness of it. *(SM: This merchant's evidence and that of the following gives the typical prices of Shetland yarn that was sold on to Lerwick merchants for knitting, and from their statements we can build a picture of typical thicknesses or qualities /categories of the yarn or 'worsted': A 'cut' for me here, is taken to be the measure of 100 threads of 2 yards each = 200 yards.* So, later, '6 cuts to the ounce' = 1200 yds per ounce = c.1/ 38NM, and '14 cuts per ounce' = 2800 yds per oz = c.1/90 NM. Once spun, the thread was wound around a wooden "niddy-noddy" [Shetland: 'reel' or 'hesp tree']to make hanks with a circumference of 2 yards; therefore, counting the threads would give the length in yards. This is to the 'Gala' = "Galashiels Count" of 300 yds = 24 oz. Unlikely, but it may be that the Report's figures are to another count. For example, Linda Fryer: p 80, has the count as 100 threads to 1 'cut' = c.100 yds. If so, this would affect the figures I give in this book, but the evidence on page 59 here, again points to it being '200 yds per cut'. *Reference: 'A Stitch in Time', page 9.)*

Baltasound, Unst, January 19, 1872, ALEXANDER SANDISON, examined.

9978. You are one of the partners of the firm of Spence & Co., and you have been so since the formation of the company in 1868?- Yes…**10,182. Have you had a good deal to do in the hosiery trade?-** Yes, I have bought a good deal of it. **10,183. I understand you buy a quantity of worsted from the spinners in Unst and sell it south?-** Yes; I generally sell it in Lerwick. **10,184. At what rates do you generally buy the worsted?-** We never like to buy anything coarser than we can give 3d. per cut for. **10,185. The weight of that, I suppose, varies?-** The weight of what we give 3d. per cut for would be about 6 cuts to the ounce. *(SM: I make that 24 x 6 = 144 Gala count - this would be what we'd class as a gossamer weight of today : 1/46NM.)* **10,186. That would be 24s. per lb.?-** Yes; but the number of ounces is not a criterion, because the less the weight the higher the price. We have given as high as 7d. per cut for worsted, and that should weigh 14 cuts of 100 threads to the ounce. That would be 8s. 2d. per ounce, or more than £7 per lb. *(SM: I make it just over £6 10s: 8s 2d is correct, that equals 98 pennies, x 16, for number of ounces in a pound = 1568d. Divide that by 240d per £ = 6.53 or just under £6/11s, which equals over £418. in 2005's RPI money terms = over £26 per oz!)* **10,187. Is not that a very high price?-** Yes; but we would give cash for any amount of that kind of worsted we could get, or for worsted at 6d. for 12 cuts to the ounce, but very few can spin that. It is a very fine thread. **10,188. Have you known much worsted sold at the rate of £7, 12s. per lb.?-** No, not very much, because there are very few who can spin it so fine. It is just like a cobweb. *(SM: I should say so, equals c1/120NM or 3875 yds per oz!)*

10,189. What quantity of worsted of that sort would it take to make a shawl of the ordinary size? About 40 cuts?- That would be a small shawl. I have put as high as 70 cuts of that fine worsted into a shawl; but that was a large shawl. The usual size is 25 to 30 scores, made out of 3d. worsted. *(SM: I definitely think we're talking Gossamer Class lace here at 600 sts a side square for an 81 inch shawl.*)*

10,190. The score refers to the size of the shawl?- Yes; twenty scores is twenty threads or twenty stitches of the needle across from side to side. **10,191. Is the size of the shawl generally measured by the score or by the yard?-** It is generally measured by the score when the girl commences to knit it. **10,192. Then a shawl of that size would take 40 cuts of that fine worsted?-** No; a *2¼ yard shawl would take 60 cuts of that fine worsted. **10,193. The worsted of such a shawl would cost £1, 15s?-** Yes. *(SM: £111.56p in 2005 RPI .)*

10,194. Can you give me any idea what the knitting of that shawl is generally put in at?- The knitting of shawl of that kind should be 25s. to 30s. *(SM: 30s = £95.62p in 2005 RPI terms.)* **10,195. Are these shawls made in Unst?-** Yes; I have got a shawl made in Unst that cost £4, and some that cost £3, and between £3 and £4. *(SM: £192/£256 RPI 2005.)* **10,196. Would the knitting cost as much in Lerwick?-** I don't know. I generally think, as a rule, that the knitter ought to get as much for her work as the price of the worsted. **10,197. But it is somewhat less than the price of the worsted in these fine shawls?-** Yes.

10,198. Suppose a shawl of which the worsted cost you 35s. and the knitting 25s. - that is £3 altogether: what would that be invoiced for to the merchant in the south?- Perhaps I am not able to give very good information upon that point, because I have always found these shawls to be a part of my stock which it was very difficult to dispose of. **10,199. Do you mean the fine shawls?-** No. I have generally got shawls of that sort made upon an order from gentlemen who happen to come down here, and I usually charge them the cost of the work and dressing, and so on; but I have found it a very difficult thing to sell hosiery.

Lerwick, January 27, 1872, MARGARET JAMIESON, examined

14,035. Do you live in Quarff?- Yes. **14,036. Are you sometimes employed in knitting?-** Yes, in knitting and dressing. I have also a little farm which I work, but I generally work at the knitting and dressing when I can get that kind of work to do. The farm is my brother's but he is very ill.

14,037. Do you knit with your own wool, or is it given out to you by the merchants?- I always knit with wool which I purchase for myself. **14,038. What kind of things do you knit?-** Shawls, veils, haps, plaids, and other things. *(SM: Here, a 'plaid' seems to be a term for a long shawl - what we'd now call a stole. Valerie Reilly describes Paisley 'plaids' of the 1820s onwards, as 10 x 5 feet (3 x 1.5m) or larger. She writes there were also three-quarter plaids - about 8 x 4 feet (2.45 x 1.2m). Generally, the square shawl was worn folded diagonally with the point hanging down the back, but the plaid was worn "folded double and square" on the shoulders: p.35 The Paisley Pattern published by Richard Drew, 1987; this would be as shown by hap on frontispiece. See also my comment on page 55.)* **14,039. Are you always paid for these in goods?-** I sold a plaid to Mr Sinclair in the spring when I was unwell, and did not get it settled for until the summer. The price of the article was 18s., *(SM: £57.37 RPI 2005.)* and I asked a halfpenny from him, and he refused to give it to me.

14,040. Did he not give you the halfpenny?- He gave it to me in the end, because I had to post a letter, and I got the halfpenny from him for that purpose. **14,041. Was the postage of that letter only a halfpenny?-** No, but I had another halfpenny of my own, and I required the halfpenny from him to buy a stamp with. On Wednesday last I sold a plaid to him for 20s. and asked 2s. in cash at the end of the settlement, but they refused to give it to me. I then asked 1s. 6d., and they said if I got that they would mark it as 1s. 9d. against me. **14,042. Who said that?-** It was one of the serving-men in Mr Sinclair's shop; I don't know his name. *(SM: Adam Tait, see below.)* Then I asked 1s., and he said it would be 1s. 3d. against me; but I refused to take it on that footing. I then asked for 9d. which he consented to give me, saying he did not have it in the shop, but that he would borrow it from one of the clerks or serving-men. **14,043. Did he say he did not have 9d. in the shop?-** Yes. I got 6d. and left 3d. due, which I could not get unless I took calico. **14,044. You did not put him to the trouble of borrowing the 9d.?-** He borrowed 4d. from one of the persons there, and he found 2d. in the counter. **14,045. Do you think there was no money in the till at that time?-** I do not know anything about it except what he told me. I consider from my own experience, and from what I hear from others, that we are very much like the Hebrews of Egypt,- very much burdened down with many things, and not able to bear our burdens. **14,046. When you took the shawl in the other day, which you sold for a pound, did you bargain that you were to get payment for it in goods?-** There was no bargain made about it. **14,047. When you sold the shawl in the previous spring, was it marked down in an account, or did you get a line for it?-** I got a line for it. *(SM: 'line' means a sort of credit note for exchange in that shop for goods at a later date. Calico is a type of woven cotton.)*

14,048. Did you send in your shawl?- No; I went in and sold it and asked a line, which I got. **14,049. Did you not want the goods at the time?-** I got some goods and the balance in a line. **14,050. But you did not want to take the whole in goods?-** No, I refused to do that. I did not want them until afterwards. **14,051. Does it often happen that you don't want goods when you sell your shawls, and that you would rather have money?-** We would rather have money, because there are many things that we require it for. There are many taxes we have to pay, and there are many things we can only buy with money. **14,052. Would you take a lower price for your hosiery if you could get cash instead of goods?-** I don't know, because goods will help us through a part of the year as well as if we got a little money. I consider our hosiery is worth what we sell it at, even although it was paid in cash.

Lerwick, January 27, 1872, ADAM TAIT, examined.

14,280. You are a shopman to Mr. Robert Sinclair?- I am. **14,281. Did you purchase a hap lately from Margaret Jamieson, Quarff, who has been examined today?**- Mr. Sinclair purchased it, and I settled with her for it the time she sold it. *(SM: Lovely, precise answer!)* **14,282. When was that?**- About three days ago. It was a long plaid she sold. **14,283. What was the price of it?**- 20s. in goods; and that was paid. **14,284. To what extent did you supply her with goods?**- I gave her 19s. 6d. worth of goods and 6d. in cash. She wanted 3s. in cash. I told her the bargain was made in goods, and I could not give it to her in cash. Besides, there was no cash in the drawer at the time. Then she thought of something else she wanted, and I borrowed 6d. from the clerk in the end gave it to her.

…..**14,287. On what day was that?**- I think it was on Wednesday last, but I am not certain, and about twelve or one o'clock in the day. I recollect the transaction very well, as the woman seemed to be ill-pleased when she went out. **14,288. Is it a frequent thing to tell a woman who asks for cash; that there is no cash in the shop?**- No; that does not often happen.

Lerwick, January 30, 1872, JOHN WALKER, recalled. *(SM: Mr Walker is an Edinburgh merchant with very strong opinions about the way the Shetland merchants transact their business. His earlier evidence was much disputed by them, he appears now to confirm his earlier points. Seems authoritative and voluble.)*

15,920. You formerly gave evidence before the Commissioners under the Act of 1870, in Edinburgh?- I did. **15,921. Are there any points on which you wish to give further information?**- I merely wish to reaffirm all that I previously stated. From what the people say, the only thing that seems to require explanation, is with regard to the value of the worsted or wool for the making of a shawl.

15,922. You refer to question 44,290: 'I know for a fact that the worsted of a shawl which sells at about 30s. is worth from 2s. to 3s. They nominally give the worker 9s. for working it, but if they get it in goods that will be about 4s.; and they get from 25s. to 30s. for it?'- Yes. The question was intended to apply to half square shawls and haps selling at from £1 to 30s., according to the verdancy of the animal that was buying it *(SM: Seems to be his term for how rich the purchaser is!)* It takes about sixteen hundreds *(SM: at '2 yards' = 3200 yds.)* to make a hap, and the worsted will be worth from 2d. to 2 ½ d. *(SM: I believe he means 'per cut' of 200 yards).* It will take from sixteen to seventeen hundreds to make a half square fine shawl, and the worsted of it will be worth about 4d. *(SM: per 'cut'? If so, he's saying the worsted would cost less than 6s. then)* and these shawls are sold at from 18s. to 30s., according as customers can be got for them.

15,923. Are haps often sold at so high a price as 30s? - No, not haps; they are sold up to about £1. That has been my experience. I may say that I have been in *(SM: Presumably 'Lerwick')* shops, when the first question asked before a price was stated was, whether the article was for the person's self or for a stranger; that is to say, was it to be sold to a person in the country, or was it to go away outside, because in these cases they have two different prices. I have likewise been in shops when, if there were any of the knitting girls there selling shawls or other articles, the merchant would take very good care to state the price to his other customers in the lowest possible voice, and at the farthest possible distance from these girls; and I have been repeatedly told that they will occasionally put the price upon a piece of paper, so as not to let the knitters hear it.

That I say in contradiction to the assertion which is made, that the merchants sell the hosiery articles at the same price as that at which they nominally buy them. Again, I want to point out that in most cases all the worsted that the hosiery merchants in Lerwick dealt in up to the last year was bought from the country merchants for goods, and therefore that even that nominal value did not represent the true value of the articles. I produce an account containing transactions amounting to £146; it is all balanced by goods, which were entirely worsted, up to £1, 3s. 10d. *(SM: sic – I think he's saying that the Lerwick merchants exchanged their goods for worsted yarn from the country merchants except for the odd £1,3/10d.)* The only item of cash I find in the account is 15s. Lately, however, they have been obliged and are ready to buy the worsted for cash, because they cannot do without it, and the supply of worsted is decreasing.

15,924. You are speaking of Shetland worsted?- Yes. I may mention also that that estimate of the value of the worsted for a shawl was intended by me to embrace the Yorkshire worsted, or what they call the Pyrenees, although I don't suppose either the worsted or the wool ever saw the Pyrenees: it is made in Yorkshire. *(SM: Now, here is a problem, he may be quoting a Bradford Yarn Count of '256 yds per lb' skeins, but why he refers to it earlier in "hundreds" I'm not sure, unless a particular weight of yarn was put up in skeins of 100 threads. Quick dip here into "Caulfield & Saward's Dictionary of Needlework" 1882, which has revealing entries that highlight the confusing descriptions of wool and yarns at the time:*

*" **Berlin Wool**, otherwise called GERMAN WOOL and ZEPHYR MERINO. – Manufactured for the purpose of knitting and embroidery. It is to be had in two sizes, the single and the double. Keighley, in Yorkshire, is the chief seat of manufacture and it is sold either in skeins or by weight. A quantity of real German wool is brought into Great Britain in a raw state, and is combed, spun, and dyed, chiefly in Scotland…………….Berlin or German wool is the finest of all descriptions of wool and is produced from the fleece of the Merino breed of Saxony sheep, and of neighbouring German states" p.27 …"but much of our best [German] wool has been……..[lately from]…… Australia" p.222*

"Woollen Yarn……. There is also the Leviathan wool, which is composed of many strands, and is full and soft,…. The Eider Yarn [Merino], which is peculiarly delicate and glossy, and employed for hand made shawls and scarves;………There is also…the Shetland wool which is finer than the latter [Berlin]; the Pyrenean, which is of a still finer description; and Zephyr wool, which is remarkably thin and fine."p.522. While I was in there, I also looked up -

"Alpaca Yarn, a very valuable description of yarn, and much superior to the ordinary qualities of sheep's wool.... It is spun so finely that the thread may be used either alone or in combination with silk or cashmere.... The seat of the English trade is at Bradford" [Yorkshire].)... p.5.........."Shetland Wool,....[SM:I think they go on to describe mill spun yarn as they go on to say:]As sold in the shops, this is a yarn much employed for the knitting of shawls....[babywear]... The yarn is exceedingly soft and has only two threads.... Wool of this kind is not produced in England proper, it is thicker than Pyrenean wool , and softer than both it and the Andalusian, not being so tightly twisted. ....the breed goes by the name of Beaver sheep." p.447. Interestingly, the entry for Andulusian Wool is as follows: "This is also called Victoria Wool, and is a fine soft warm make of woolen thread or yarn,....it is the same wool as the Shetland, but is thicker, being spun with four threads instead of two." p.6. So to sum up, there seems little distinction between a wool's origin, and count in these references, the name of a yarn is a description of its thickness and not necessarily of its origin, but this may reflect more on the compilers of that book.)

15,925. Are you speaking, in both these cases of haps and of shawls, of articles made of Shetland worsted?- All the haps are made from Shetland worsted, the coarser worsted. **15,926. You said in that answer to which you have referred, 'They nominally give the worker 9s. for working it, but if they get it in goods that will be about 4s.:' is not that a little too strong?-** I don't think it. *(SM: Excellent man! Concise answer, possibly his shortest and therefore the most eloquent one for that; I get a feeling he's a bit of a performer but truly, he's 'A Hero', like Sheriff Guthrie! Wish I could give all Mr Walker's evidence regarding quality of Shetland goods, trade and so on but space limits us here.)*

15,927. That assumes that the charge for the goods is about 100 per cent. above the cost price, or rather it assumes that it is 100 per cent. above the price at which the worker of the shawl ought to get these goods, which would not be the cost price, but the retail price?- No, I don't mean that. I mean to say that if these merchants were to go to the proper market, they could buy their goods at such a rate that they would be able to sell them at 100 per cent. profit; but I know that a great many of these merchants go to second-hand houses to buy. Whether it is for the object of getting long credits, or what it is, I don't know; but I know from the parties who come here that a great many of them are not first-class houses….. Wholesale houses in Aberdeen are not in the same position as wholesale houses in London.

Lerwick, February 5, 1872, Mrs. JOAN WINWICK or FORDYCE, examined.

16,038. Do you live in Chromate Lane, Lerwick?-Yes. **16,039. Is your husband alive?-**Yes. He is a pensioner. He was a carpenter to trade, but he does nothing now. **16,040. Do you knit worsted work?-** Yes, I knit, but for myself only. I knit with my own wool, and sell the goods.

16,041. Have you never knitted with merchants' wool?- No. **16,042. To whom do you generally sell your hosiery?-** I always sold it to Mr. Robert Sinclair since he became a merchant. I always knit haps or coarse shawls.

16,043. What do you pay for the worsted which you use in knitting?- When I buy the worsted it is 2d. per hundred *(SM: equals a 'cut'.)* ; but when I buy the wool and spin it myself, it comes to be a great deal dearer. We cannot get proper worsted to buy, and we have to manufacture it with our own hands. **16,044. Is the worsted which you buy at 2d. per hundred the kind which you use for a hap of ordinary quality?-**Yes.

16,045. At what price do you sell a hap two yards in size made of that worsted?- Perhaps about 10s.

16,046. Have you any of these haps in hand just now?- No. **16,047. Have you sold any lately?-** No; I have not sold any this winter. I have not been knitting this winter to sell. I have just been doing things for my own family. **16,048. What else have you knitted besides haps?-** I have knitted nothing but haps for a good while. Since I could not see to do finer work I have been spinning worsted and making frocks for my husband, and stockings and things of that sort. **16,049. Where do you buy your worsted?-** I have not bought any worsted for a long time. I always bought the wool and spun it myself, because I could not get the worsted to buy.

16,050. Where did you buy your wool? - I buy skins from the women who sell the sheep, and get the wool ru'ed *(SM: 'rooed')* off the sheep when they are killed. **16,051. Are there women who go about and sell wool in that way?-** They sell mutton, but they will sell wool to us when we go to their houses and ask them for it. **16,052. Do these women buy the whole sheep?-** Yes, they buy them alive; and when they have killed them, they sell the mutton to any person in the town who will buy it. **16,053. Are there many such women?-** I suppose there are a few, but I cannot say how many. **16,054. Is that the way in which many people get their supply of wool for spinning?-** I think it is, because we cannot get wool in any other way.

16,055. How much wool do you buy at a time?- I have bought 10s. or 12s. worth at a time,- just the skin as I could get it. **16,056. How much do you think you pay for the wool per lb. in that way?-** I have seen it cost me 2s. and 16d. and 18d.; but it has been higher of late since the wool became so dear.

16,057. Is not that a very high price for it?- Yes. **16,058. Is it not more commonly about 1s. per lb.?-** Yes. When I came to Lerwick it was 1s., 8d., and 6d. **16,059. Is it not still to be got at 1s. per lb.?-** Perhaps it may be in country places, where they have plenty of it; but I cannot get it for 1s. unless it is very coarse, and a great deal of refuse *(SM: 'refuse' = "rubbish" – tiny burrs, "taggles" etc.)* in it. **6,060. How much wool does it take to make a hap two yards square?-** About 2 lbs. That would be 16 hundreds or cuts. **16,061. Are you speaking all this time of a hap of the ordinary quality?-** Yes, the ordinary quality. *(SM: So '8 cuts' would = 16 ozs & '1 cut of 200 yds' would weigh 2 oz. Therefore, the yarn is 100 yds per oz = c1/3.3NM, very close to that of the Morag at a 1/3.7NM equivalent, so Morag is made in slightly finer yarn.)*

16,062. Do you know what a woman gets for knitting a hap of that kind when it is given out?- I cannot say exactly; but I think they give some knitters for plain work only 2d. per hundred, or perhaps a little more. That is what they say they get for knitting plain work. **16,063. Do they count the payment of the knitting by hundreds?-** I suppose some of them do, but I have never put out any to knit myself, or taken any in to knit.

16,064. Then for a hap like that, if there were 16 hundreds in it, the knitter would get only 2s. 8d. *(SM: £8.50 RPI 2005)* **for the knitting?-** Yes; but I think that for knitting borders they get a little more. It is for plain frocks that they say they get 2d. per hundred. **16,065. Are you always paid in goods for your work?-** Mr. Sinclair always gave me what I asked. When I asked a little money I got it, and when I required goods for my family, such as soap, soda, or tea, I got them too. **16,066. But I suppose it was understood that you were to be paid in goods?-** Yes, that was the custom of the place; but he always trusted me with anything I wanted, if I happened to be due him something at times.

Lerwick, February 5, 1872, Mrs. ROSINA DUNCAN or SMITH, examined.

16,067. Do you live in Lerwick?- Yes. **16,068. Is your husband alive?-** Yes. He is turning an old man now, but he was at the sea at one time. **16,069. Has he got a pension?-** No. **16,070. Do you employ yourself in knitting?-** I knit a little for my own family. **16,071. Have you given up knitting for other people?-** Yes.

16,072. Did you knit for Mr. Sinclair at one time?- I sold him a few haps last year. **16,073. Did you sell him a great number before that-** I did not; but when I had any little things I sold them to Mr. Joseph Leask, and got money articles *(SM: This is their term for essentials: lamp oil, corn, groceries, wool – goods that the merchants insisted on cash sales only)* for them.

16,074. Did you ever sell so many as half a dozen to Sinclair?- I cannot say, for I did not count them. The last one I sold was to him. **16,075. What did you get for it?-** 12s. *(SM: about £38 in 2005 terms, and she supplied her own worsted!)*

16,076. How much wool was in it?- I cannot say, for I spun it myself, and wrought it until it was done. **16,077. Do you not know how many cuts of worsted were in it?-** No; I did not count them. **16,078. What was the size of it?-** I suppose it would be about two yards. **16,079. Was it made of fine wool or ordinary wool?-** It was just the ordinary wool that is used for haps. **16,080. Were you paid in money or in goods for it?-** I was paid mostly in goods, but he gave me money without my asking for it.

(SM: This seemed to me to be a quick answer, one felt this witness either did not want to offend Mr Sinclair, or that he may have been an exceptional merchant. Actual coin was rarely given for haps or the coarser items of hosiery, usually only the finest knitters of lace could ask for and get cash, the others were lucky to get pence or shillings and often had to explain why they wouldn't take merchant's goods. Sometimes a 'line' or credit note, was taken which could be traded quietly and usually at a discount, for cash with other Shetlanders.)

16,081. How much money did you get?- 1s. or so. I could not exactly say how much, but he gave me what I required. I got the goods which I required, and he gave me that money, and he also gave me tea, which was the same as money, because if I had had to buy it I would have had to pay for it. **16,082. Could you get money for the tea?-** I did not sell it; I kept it for my own use.

(SM: Also, the goods knitters got were frequently exchanged with others out of town such as local farmers, for meat or corn etc. again normally at a less favourable rate for them.. Though the barter system was officially 'penal' – illegal, the evidence Sheriff Guthrie is collating proves that it was widespread in Shetland, and his admirable work did help towards mitigating some of the effects of the truck system but it continued long afterwards. Evidence from both knitters and merchant traders seems to show that they know it was a prohibited system.) **16,083. Did you ever sell anything that you got for hosiery?-** No. I always required anything I got for my own family.

Lerwick, February 5, 1872, ELIZABETH MALCOMSON, recalled.

16,093. Do you live with your mother in Baker's Close, Lerwick?- Yes. **16,094. What do you do?-** I sometimes knit, and sometimes sew; but I mostly knit. My mother knits sometimes, and does the house-work.

16,095. Do you support yourself mostly by knitting?-Yes, almost entirely. **16,096. What kind of knitting do you do?-** Fine veils and shawls. ....**16,113. What is the usual price that you get for your fine shawls?-** We generally get 10s. or 12s., but that is not the very finest worsted either. **16,114. Are these shawls knitted with the merchant's worsted?-** Yes. **16,115. It is always given out to you, and you keep an account?-** Yes.

16,116. Do you know what quality of worsted it is that you knit one of these shawls with?- It is usually Shetland worsted. The price of it is 3½ d., and some of it 4d. per cut; at least I would think so, judging by the fineness of the worsted. **16,117. Have you sometimes bought worsted yourself?-** Yes, sometimes. **16,118. Have you bought it often enough to know the quality and price?-** Yes. **16,119. What size of shawl is it that you get 12s. for?-**About 2¼ yards. That, is, 25 scores on each border and there are four borders in the square. **16,120. Then you could say quite positively that for a shawl of 25 scores, knitted with 3½ d. worsted, and measuring 2¼ yards, you got 12s. in goods?-** Yes.

(SM: Finally, we can get an idea of the yarn used: the shawl measures 81 inches square, there are a maximum of 500 sts per border – 'score' = '20'; in quite a thick worsted which would be perhaps a 2/14NM or Shetland lace- weight/ equivalent of around 200 yds per ounce, this would be a larger version of the 2 ply Grey Shawl pictured page 42.) **16,121. Do you ever sell shawls to any persons except the merchants?-** No.

Lerwick, February 5, 1872, Mrs. MARGARET SMITH or GIFFORD, examined.

16,203. Do you live in Lerwick?- Yes. **16,204. Do you knit haps?-** Yes; but only a few, because I am getting old and weak, and I am not so able to work as I used to be. **16,205. Have you knitted lately for Mr. Sinclair?-** I have knitted for him for a long time. I think it is about a fortnight since I sold my last hap to him. It was between 1½ and 1¾ yards. **6,206. What kind of wool was it made of?-** Just common wool of different kinds - grey and black and white. **16,207. Was it worth about 2d. per hundred?-** It would be worth about that. *(SM: Sounds again, like a 'Shetland 2000' equivalent as the price is comparatively low; though that might reflect on the bargaining for the yarn itself.)*

16,208. What did you sell it for?- 6s.; that was what I commonly got for these little haps. **16,209. Did you sell it for that price in goods?-** I was to get anything I wanted. I have something to get yet. I got tea and soap, or anything I required, and I shall get the rest as I need it. **16,210. Was that about the ordinary price which you got for a hap of that size and quality?-**Yes. If I could make them bigger, I would get more money, perhaps 10s., and from that down to 6s. **16,211. How long have you been dealing with Mr. Sinclair?-** I have dealt with him from 1840 or 1845. **16,212. Have you always been paid by him in goods during that time?-** Yes, when I asked them; but if I asked any other thing I got whatever I asked. **16,213. Have you bought articles for money in Mr. Sinclair's shop?-** It was not very often that he got any money from us; but when I wanted anything from him, I found there was no difference whether I paid for it in money or in goods.

Selected Extracts from Sheriff Guthrie's Summaries

KNITTING PAID IN GOODS / TWO PRICES FOR GOODS / MERCHANTS PRICES FOR GOODS

"Although payment in goods, or in account, of work done with the merchants' wool may be held to be an offence under the existing law, the custom of barter has so long existed in Shetland, and is so thoroughly interwoven with the habits of the people, that the question has never been raised in the local courts, and it does not even appear to have occurred to merchants that they might be held to infringe the law. In regard to both branches of the trade, the sale or barter of the knitted articles, and the employment of women to knit them, evidence has been freely given by the merchants themselves. In both branches of the trade, it is the custom and understanding of the country, from Unst to Dunrossness, that payment shall be made in goods. Formerly money payment was never thought of. ….There is no doubt that the general prices of tea and drapery goods are higher where hosiery is dealt in. It may be that a cash purchaser gets a reduction occasionally, or always if it is asked for. But there is a general concurrence of testimony to the effect that goods got by knitters at the hosiery shops are dearer than at other shops in Shetland. Various merchants admit that a higher profit is charged, in consequence of the custom of paying in hosiery. …………But while the merchants assert that they have no direct profit upon their sales of knitted goods, or at least none but the smallest, they do not deny that, in order to repay themselves for the trouble and risk involved in the two transactions upon which this profit is realized, they charge considerably more for their tea and drapery goods than the ordinary retail price in other districts. In other words, although there is nominally no profit upon the knitted goods, there is a double profit, or a very large profit, on the drapery goods, tea, etc., bartered for it. If, therefore, we calculate what the price of these goods should be at the ordinary retail rate, and deduct the surplus from the nominal price of the knitted articles, we find that the usual percentage of profit is obtained on the latter as well as on the tea and drapery."

SALE OF GOODS GOT FOR KNITTING

"With many women money is a necessity for payment of rent, purchase of provisions, and other purposes. Cotton goods, tea, and shoes, which are almost the only things they can get for their knitting, are not enough to keep life in them. Those who depend entirely on their own labour have therefore to find some other means of providing themselves with these necessaries; and it is chiefly by them that the complaints of the present system are made. Some work out-of-doors for part of the year, <e.g.> in fish-curing or farm-work. In many cases they have sold the goods obtained at the shop, or bartered them with neighbours, for potatoes or meal. This practice cannot be described as universal, because the greater number of knitters live with parents, or have some supplementary occupation by which they get money. But still the practice is proved to have been so common that the ignorance which many witnesses profess with regard to its existence is surprising. Tea especially is a sort of currency with which knitters obtain supplies of provisions. Even if there were not direct testimony to this effect, it would be a fair inference from the large quantities of tea which the pass-books and merchants' books show that they get. Thus, in one account, more than a half of the total amount consists of ¼ lb. packages of tea.

"Cotton and drapery goods are also sold or exchanged by knitters in order to get provisions or wool, and sometimes at a considerable loss. Thus Isabella Henderson says she had to give goods which cost 6s. 6d. for 5s. worth of meal. Women at Scalloway stated that they had frequently hawked the goods given them for knitting through the country for meal and potatoes. Mary Coutts says: '11,601. How do you get your provisions, such as meal and potatoes?- We give tea to the farmers, and get meal and potatoes for it. We have sometimes to go to the west side, to Walls and Sandness, for that. Our aunt, Elizabeth Coutts, has done that for us. She has not been to Walls and Sandness for the last two years, …..'" *(SM: As said earlier, it is taken to be a true account of the Truck system, which lingered on until the mid 20th century. There regretfully, we must leave this report with gratitude for the insights it provides into the life of the knitters of Shetland.)*

Chart Symbols

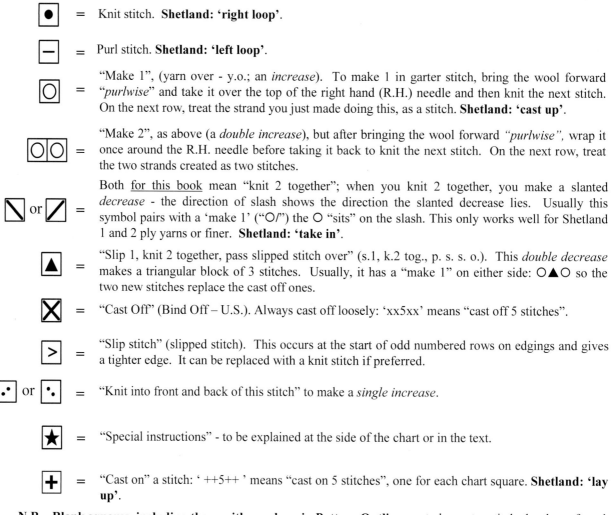

●	=	Knit stitch. **Shetland: 'right loop'.**
−	=	Purl stitch. **Shetland: 'left loop'.**
O	=	"Make 1", (yarn over - y.o.; an *increase*). To make 1 in garter stitch, bring the wool forward *"purlwise"* and take it over the top of the right hand (R.H.) needle and then knit the next stitch. On the next row, treat the strand you just made doing this, as a stitch. **Shetland: 'cast up'.**
O O	=	"Make 2", as above (a *double increase*), but after bringing the wool forward *"purlwise"*, wrap it once around the R.H. needle before taking it back to knit the next stitch. On the next row, treat the two strands created as two stitches.
╲ or ╱	=	Both <u>for this book</u> mean "knit 2 together"; when you knit 2 together, you make a slanted *decrease* - the direction of slash shows the direction the slanted decrease lies. Usually this symbol pairs with a 'make 1' ("O/") the O "sits" on the slash. This only works well for Shetland 1 and 2 ply yarns or finer. **Shetland: 'take in'.**
▲	=	"Slip 1, knit 2 together, pass slipped stitch over" (s.1, k.2 tog., p. s. s. o.). This *double decrease* makes a triangular block of 3 stitches. Usually, it has a "make 1" on either side: O▲O so the two new stitches replace the cast off ones.
✕	=	"Cast Off" (Bind Off – U.S.). Always cast off loosely: 'xx5xx' means "cast off 5 stitches".
>	=	"Slip stitch" (slipped stitch). This occurs at the start of odd numbered rows on edgings and gives a tighter edge. It can be replaced with a knit stitch if preferred.
⸫ or ⸪	=	"Knit into front and back of this stitch" to make a *single increase*.
★	=	"Special instructions" - to be explained at the side of the chart or in the text.
✚	=	"Cast on" a stitch: ' ++5++ ' means "cast on 5 stitches", one for each chart square. **Shetland: 'lay up'.**

N.B. Blank squares, including those with numbers in Pattern Outline are to be garter stitched - also referred to as *plain knitted*. **In Shetland, plain knit rows were called 'riggies'.** *(ref: C Brown.)*

Knitting Cast On

Put a stitch on the LH needle, *knit into it and put new stitch on LH needle**. Repeat from * to ** until you have the correct number of stitches on LH needle. This makes an elastic cast on edge.

Knitting Tips and Aftercare:

Always remember to **knit to the end of a row** before finishing. Primarily, this is so you keep the tension of the row even - but it also means that you start the next session with a fresh row and fresh pattern line on the chart.
Obviously, you will knit with clean hands, but it really helps any knitting you are doing if you also regularly dust your hands with **talcum powder** when knitting - I keep a small container of baby powder in my knitting bag. Doing this helps the stitches to glide smoothly along the needles and so helps with knitting tension, as well as stopping the stitches from bunching or jamming together which they frequently can do, when the weather and you are hot. The talc washes out in the finishing process.

When you have finished, **keep any remaining wool together with the pattern** so that if the worst should happen and the shawl needs a repair, these are at hand. I keep them with the stored shawl in a clean pillowcase at the top of the airing cupboard – away from any possible leaks! A good idea is to parcel the shawl in white, acid-free tissue paper and if you suspect you may have a moth problem, store lavender scented soap bars nearby as a deterrent. Anyway, inspect the shawl yearly, should you want to use it - and it's not necessary to redress it - simply lay the unfolded shawl on the double bed or suitable large flat surface and give it a light coating of spray starch and hand-smooth out the creases, then leave to dry. Normally, this takes only a few minutes to half an hour, you could re-pin an area if you need to for this.

Mending Should the shawl get holed, secure all loose stitches onto a pin or thread as soon as possible. Use the pattern and saved yarn to repair the damage. Always do mending before washing.
Words in italics on this page are the technical knitting terms – see *Heirloom Knitting*.